EMPOWERMENT OF WOMEN IN PANCHAYATI RAJ INSTITUTIONS

EMPOWERMENT OF WOMEN IN PANCHAYATI RAJ INSTITUTIONS

ANUPAMA PURI MAHAJAN

ANAMIKA PUBLISHERS & DISTRIBUTORS (P) LTD.
4697/3, 21A, Ansari Road, Daryaganj, New Delhi-110002
Phones: 23281655, 23270239; Fax: 011-27868035
e-mail: anamikapublishers@yahoo.co.in

First Published 2012

ISBN 978-81-7975-399-6

PRINTED IN INDIA

Published by Anamika Publishers & Distributors (P) Ltd., 4697/3, 21A, Ansari Road, Daryaganj, New Delhi 110002. Typset by Shivani Computer, Shahdara Delhi 110092 and Printed at Nagri Printers, Delhi.

CONTENTS

Dedicated

to

SHREE JEE

PREFACE

It is a known fact that the concept of local government or panchayat has filtered down from the Vedic times. At the grass root level, the village was an economic as well as an administrative unit. The villages and their administrative system are intact today also with some minor variations.

Presently, local government in India consists of two broad categories—Rural and Urban—as a result of constitutional amendments in 1992. Full benefit of development can be realized only with full participation. The role of women cannot be isolated from the total framework of development as they constitute half of the population. A review of the economic roles played by women in India shows that the traditional village community of India which consisted of the cultivators, the artisans and those performing menial tasks consisted chiefly of women. They played a distinctive and accepted role in the process of earning a livelihood for the family in both the marketing of products of agriculture and handicrafts.

Since the decade of women (1975-85), women's development has been conceptualized by equity, empowerment and rights-based approaches with emphasis on the strategic needs of women. The "Welfare Approach", no doubt, benefitted the women as the net recipients but were not participants in the agencies and programmes created for their own development. Then came the "Empowerment Approach" through which an effort was made to eliminate gender bias by making women a part of their own development schemes and projects.

In the Constituent Assembly of 1950, as well as, the 1974 Equality Report, women leaders rejected the notion of 'Quota' in the political decision-making process. After a decade, the National Perspective Plan (1988-2000) recommended a 30 per cent seat reservation for women in Panchayats. Finally, the 73rd and 74th Amendment Acts (1992) had a provision of reserving not less than 33% per cent of the total seats for women, both at the functionary as well as membership level. Within a span of 10-15 years, more than six million women have come to active politics as a result of reservation of seats in the local government institutions.

This book aims to examine the issues related to women empowerment in P.R.I.s in Himachal Pradesh. The various topics under the lens will be the emergence and growth of P.R.I.s; an analysis of their organizational structure; to assess the educational, political and socio-economic background of the women leaders of H.P. P.R.I.s; study of the existing relationship between the Executive and women leaders; an evaluation of the role of women leaders in making the P.R.I.s programmes a success; a critical evaluation of factors impeding better performance of women leaders and finally studying the ways and means to strengthen P.R.I.s.

ACKNOWLEDGEMENT

At the outset, let me take this opportunity to express my earnest indebtedness to Professor Shiv Raj Singh, Department of Public Administration, Himachal Pradesh University, Shimla for the guidance and time he allotted to me, the patience with which he dealt with all my problems and for inspiring me with his zeal for research.

I am thankful to all the members of teaching faculty in the Department of Public Administration, Himachal Pradesh University, Shimla for their kind help. I am also thankful to Late Prof. S.L. Kaushik, Ex-Chairman, Department of Public Administration, Chandigarh, who inspired and encouraged me to carry out research in this field and late Dr. P.P.S. Gill for his moral support.

I would like to record my gratitude to my friend Mr. R.K. Bhota, Editor and P.I.O. in the Directorate of Panchayati Raj, Government of Himachal Pradesh, Tara Chand and Vinod Kumar Research Scholars, H.P. University, Shimla for helping me in collection of data. I also extend my thanks to Sh. Neem Chand for typing this manuscript. I am also thankful to the staff members of the H.P. University of Centre for Women Development Studies, Panjab University. My family has been like elixir to me who have been an incessant and true support for me during the period of study. The person whom I want to thank first is being mentioned the last. I record sincere thanks to my husband Dr. S.K. Mahajan, Professor, Department of Public Administration, H.P. University, Shimla for his guidance and support. I also owe my thanks to my parents and parents-in-law for their deep understanding and encouragement. Last but never the least, I thank my daughters

Pawini and Vansha for the patience and support that they extended to me to accomplish this work.

Shimla Anupama Puri Mahajan

ABBREVIATIONS

C.D.	:	Community Development
C.D.P.	:	Community Development Programme
G.P.	:	Gram Panchayat
H.P.	:	Himachal Pradesh
H.P. P.R. Act	:	Himachal Pradesh Panchayati Raj Act.
I.R.D.P.	:	Integrated Rural Development Programme
M.L.A.	:	Member of Legislative Assembly
M.P.	:	Member of Parliament
N.E.S.	:	National Extension Service
O.B.Cs.	:	Other Backward Classes
P.R.	:	Panchayati Raj
P.R.I.	:	Panchayati Raj Institutions
S.Cs.	:	Scheduled Castes
S.Ts.	:	Scheduled Tribes
V.I.Ps.	:	Very Important Persons

1. INTRODUCTION

The Panchayati Raj is an ancient concept which has a long history in India. The elements of Panchayats existed even in the ancient period. In this way, these are the oldest administrative institutions in the country. "The tradition of having Panchayats has been one of the fundamental concepts of Indian Culture". If we go into the historical context of P.R. system, we will find that the system has been existing in India since the ancient Vedic periods. In Vedic age, the village was looked after by a person who was known as 'Gramini'. Likewise, in the periods of Mauryas and Guptas, references are found of a village and a district respectively. The Mauryan and Gupta administration provided a systematic base to the P.R. system. During the Mughal administration, Panchayats used to perform works relating to administrative, social and economic development.[1] Panchayats have been the backbone of the Indian villages since the beginning of the recorded history.[2] PRI is a real local self-government, providing an opportunity to local people, adequate and sufficient powers and resources to equip them solve the local problems. During Vedic era powers vested in the hands of people and the organization was known as 'Panchayat System'.[3]

Description of Panchayats is available in famous books such as *Jatakas*, *Ramayana* and Kautilya's *Arthashastra*.[4] One can find reference of local administration in the early Vedic times when the villagers themselves managed the simple affairs of the village. As it can be found in the work of Kautilya, it seemed that the villages were completely self-governing originally and were practically free from central control. As time passed by, they were brought under control of the king after which the village assembly lost much of its power and prestige. Some local matters, however, continued to be decided by this assembly. It was a popular body consisting of elders of the village. The headman was the president of the village assembly. Presumably, he was the leader of both civil and military purposes of village. Also, it was the connecting link between the village and central administration. There is no mention of the Municipal Board or its committees by Kautilya.

However, the village governments established by tradition were not exactly democratic in character. The institution of local self-governments received considerable attention during the British rule but the focus was essentially on the urban local bodies. It is only after independence that the debates over Mahatma Gandhi's vision of Gram Swaraj led to a consensus and a provision was made in the Constitution under the Directive Principles of State Policy in Article 40, which reads, "The state shall take steps to organize village Panchayats and endow them with such powers and authority as may be necessary to enable them to function as units of self-governments".[5]

In the beginning, there was no mention of Panchayati Raj in the Draft Constitution. However, this happened in the final draft, the persons imbued with Gandhian Philosophy were able to include Panchayati Raj in Article 40 of the Indian Constitution. Also, the state legislatives have been empowered under Article 246 to enact any law regarding any aspect of local self-government and now it has become a compulsion that the state governments must ensure the proper functioning for the rural bodies.

As a result, Jawaharlal Nehru while inaugurating the conference of ministers on local self-governments in the provinces in 1948, said that local self-governments is and must be the basis of any true system of democracy. We have got rather into the habit of thinking of democracy at the top and not so much below. Democracy at the top may not be a success unless you build the foundation from below.[6] The leaders of the Indian struggle for freedom were, from quite an early stage, acutely conscious of strangulating control and supervision exercised over local bodies by the state governments and the demand for enhanced local autonomy had been incorporated in their political agenda. G.K. Gokhale, an eminent liberal Congress leader, had made out an appeal for decentralization of greater powers to the rural local bodies even in 1908 when he testified before the Hobboure Commission. Later, Dr. Annie Besant, in her presidential speech at the Cultural Congress in 1917, had made scathing criticism of the Royal Commission's recommendation that the Village Panchayats should be completely under the "age and hand" of the district authorities. At the same session, another veteran leader, Surendra Nath Bannerjee also strongly attacked the British policy with regard to development of local self-government institutions in India and observed: "The government has emasculated the institution of local self-government by imposing upon them restrictions and disabilities (cries of shame)."[7] This demand for greater autonomy for rural local governing units gained support and strength later from Mahatma Gandhi which he emphasized for on the lines of ancient India's Panchayat System.

GOKHALE ON VILLAGE PANCHAYATS

The Government of India turned deaf ears not only to the resolutions passed by the Indian National Congress but to all the pious recommendations made by the Decentralization Commission appointed by it in 1907. The recommendations remained only on paper though one more member was added in 1911 to the Viceroy's council holding the portfolio of education and local self-government. Eminent leaders like Gokhale and Pherozeshah Mehta vigorously adopted a policy of political progress based on local self-government. While speaking in the Imperial Legislative Council on 13th March,

1912, Gokhale complained that the district administration continued to be where it was carried by Ripon about 30 years ago.[8] He further said, "I agree entirely with the recommendations made by the Decentralization Commission that steps should now be taken to create Village Panchayats in selected villages throughout India. I also agree that steps should be taken to establish what they call 'sub-district' Boards in those provinces where they do not at present exist". One essential condition of the success of local self-government is that those who take part in it possess a personal knowledge of the area under their management or at any rate should be able to acquire that knowledge without much difficulty. This condition cannot be fulfilled in regard to District Boards as our districts are so large. Therefore, our real local self-government should start with the village and stop with sub-districts. The District Boards may exercise only general supervisory and coordinating functions and then if the government chooses, the other functions of an advisory character might gradually be transferred to them.[9]

The reorganization of local self-government system in rural areas has been long overdue. The municipal authorities were first set up in urban areas. The Government of India Resolution of 1882, for the first time, directed local governments to set up rural boards similar to Municipal Boards. It further directed that the unit of administration should be small—the sub division, tehsil or taluka. Next, came the Report of the Decentralization Commission in 1909 which had been appointed in 1907 to enquire into the financial and administrative relations of the Government of India and the provincial governments and of 'authorities subordinate to them' and to report 'whether by measure of decentralization or otherwise' the system of government could be simplified and improved. The Commission for the first time, emphasized the importance of village organization and insisted on universal establishment of Taluka and Tehsil Boards as the principal agencies of local government. Villages continued to be neglected and District Boards were retained as principal local self-governing institutions in the rural sector.[10]

Later, Gram Panchayats were set up. The two main areas of focus (i) Provisionalisation of several functions of District Boards and (ii) Growth and development of Gram Panchayats brought about a situation in which District Boards could not be continued for long. Mahatma Gandhi emphasized that the last man should be the first to benefit, i.e., the philosophy of *Antyodaya*. This thinking comes very much near to the target group approach, in which a specific group is taken for in-depth studies and plan priorities are accordingly modified, as end is the same though means differ. Here, development of an area is not measured by its gross product on the per capita but by the rate at which the weaker sections of the population of a region grow. The development system produces a client-oriented design and the ultimate goal is to transfer all the responsibility of planning and development to the clientele themselves.[11]

After independence, development through community participation was envisaged. Two programmes—Community Development and National Extension Services were launched in 1952 and 1953 respectively but they failed to achieve their development objectives.

However, proposals of the Planning Commission for the Second Five Year Plan stressed the need for creating within the district a well organized democratic structure of administration in which village Panchayats would be organically linked with popular organizations at higher levels. The proposal was subsequently taken up by the Study Team appointed by the Committee on Planned Projects and was presided over by Balwantrai Mehta, which submitted an elaborate report in 1957.[12]

The Mehta Study Team, realizing the importance of popular participation, recommended creation of institutions which were to be statutory, elective, comprehensive in duties and functions and have enough autonomy and freedom. The creation of Panchayati Raj in 1959 with the object of interesting the authority and responsibility for rural development to rural people was held not only as an innovation but also as a revolution. Indian leaders took vigorous steps to fulfil the aim of the Constitution through planning and community development.

With the help of Ford Foundation, 15 pilot projects started functioning in India in early 1952 to improve the pathetic conditions of rural masses. In the meantime, an Indo-U.S. Technical Cooperation Agreement was signed in January, 1952, which started the first scientific and systematic programme of Community Development in India.[13]

The Community Development Programme (C.D.P.) under the Indo-US Operational Agreement was started on October 2nd, 1952, with 55 community development projects. Each of the 55 projects was to cover about three development blocks or 300 villages and a population of about three lakhs.[14] On the suggestion of the enquiry committee set up to look into the causes of failure of the 'Grow More Food' Campaign, Government of India introduced another programme called the National Extension Service (N.E.S.) on October 2nd, 1953.[15]

The Committee observed that the C.D.P. and N.E.S. programmes had failed to evoke popular initiative that local bodies at the level higher than the Panchayat had not come into the field of C.D. in any significant way. The team came to the conclusion, so long as we do not discover or create a representative and democratic institution which will supply the local interest, supervision and care necessary to ensure that expenditure of money upon local objects conforms to the needs and wishes of the locality, we will never be able to evoke local interest and excite local initiative in the field of development.[16]

The basic principles emphasized by the Committee were:

1. There should be a three-tier structure of local self-governing bodies from the village to the district, with

organic linkage among them, well defined and practical.
2. Adequate administrative powers may be entrusted to these bodies to avoid excessive state control.
3. There should be real transfer of power and responsibilities to them so that they can discharge their responsibilities.
4. Adequate resources should be transferred to the new bodies to enable them to discharge their responsibilities.
5. All development programmes should be executed through these bodies.
6. The system evolved should aim at further devolution and disposal of responsibilities in the future in the real sense.
7. State Governments should not duplicate their functioning.[17]

The study team also recommended that such a body, if created, has to be statutory, elective and equipped with the necessary executive machinery and in possession of adequate resources. It must not be cramped by too much control by the government or by government agencies. It also stated that this body can develop programmes which are of exclusive interest for the areas. In such matters, the state government will cease to operate within the area and in special circumstances when it has to do through the agency of this local body.[18]

The Balwant Rai Mehta Study Team visualized that the Panchayati Raj bodies should be made responsible for planning and development within their jurisdiction and emphasized that these bodies will be able to function effectively only if there is "devolution of power and decentralization of machinery" and thereby sought to inject an element of autonomy in their working. It also said that the backward community has to develop on so many different lines and its felt needs are so numerous and so fast growing that with limitations of available resources, it has to prescribe for itself certain properties. In a large country, with its planning for its overall development, the development of the community has to be integrated with the development of the country as a whole and added that "such integration will need that the overall priorities should be prescribed by the government and the details worked out by the village community".[19]

So, these Panchayati Raj Institutions (P.R.Is.) became mainly executive agencies for the national and state plans. The idea of decentralization was again reiterated in the Third Five Year Plan and it was proposed that the states should formulate their annual plans at least in the following activities on the basis of district and block level plans[20]: Agriculture, development of cooperatives, village industries, elementary education, rural water supply, conclusion of approach roads. Undoubtedly, the Balwantrai Mehta Committee was confronted with the problem of how to lay down some uniform lines of P.R. in view of the vast size and varying social, political and economic conditions prevailing in various parts of the country. It was thus properly visualized by the Mehta Committee and wisely endorsed by the National Development Council to take into view broad patterns of the scheme without sticking the idea of a rigid uniformity that would have made their job not only tedious but impossible as well. As a result, the Government of India did not insist that every state should follow the same pattern.[21]

In 1957, Madras government started, on an experimental basis, a pilot block of democratic decentralization in its own way, while Andhra Pradesh introduced it in twenty selected blocks, one in each district but Rajasthan was the first to give practical shape to this scheme throughout the state. Pandit Jawaharlal Nehru inaugurated it in Rajasthan on Mahatma Gandhi's birthday on October 2, 1961. As on March 31, 1984, there were 2,17,319 Gram Panchayats covering 5,61,135 villages and about 95 per cent of the rural populations, 4,526 Panchayat Samitis and 297 Zila Parishads.[22]

The development of P.R., therefore, can be said to be the logical outcome of the C.D.P. P.R. Harison has described P.G., as the most important potential invention of independent India, With the rise of P.R. (Panchayati Raj), a new phase of local government was ushered in the democratic decentralization to make the lower units of administration more popularly elected, more socially broad based and more engaged in the wider range of activities than hitherto.[23]

After the implementation of Balwant Rai Mehta Committee's recommendations, P.R. in India, in a short span, has passed through four distinct phases. The first phase (1959-1964) of ascendancy witnessed an important landmark in the history of P.R. The basic pillars of P.R. were erected in a conclusive and future-oriented style during this period. On January 12, 1958, the National Development Council endorsed the recommendations of the Mehta Committee. Thereupon, the Central Council of the Local Self-Government at its fifth meeting held at Hyderabad in 1959, took stock of the action taken by the states to implement the decision of the N.D.C. At this stage it recommended, "while the broad pattern and fundamental may be uniform there should not be any rigidity in the pattern. In fact the country is so large and P.R. is so complex a subject with far reaching consequences that there is the fullest scope of trying out various patterns and alternatives. What is most important is genuine transfer of power to the people. If this is ensured, form and pattern may necessarily vary according to conditions prevailing in different states. [24]

After the phase of ascendancy (1959-64), the P.R.I.'s witnessed the phase of stagnation from 1965-1969. Unfortunately no serious attempts or efforts were made neither to revamp nor to revitalise the P.R. structure. Since mid-sixties, the P.R. has been in a low profit. As a form of local government, it has fallen out of favour every where, except in Maharashtra and Gujarat, where it has been relatively more successful. The stagnation is the result of four major factors.

The new national and state level leadership which emerged around 1966 had much thinner links with the ideals of Mahatma Gandhi and thus much weaker ideological commitment to P.R. Secondly, the mounting food shortage of this period and the crop failures of 1966-67 led to reshuffling of priorities in the community development programme itself, resulting in an over-riding emphasis on agricultural production. In the process, a comprehensive concept of internal development got of a major project for agricultural production. Thirdly, the trend of Indian political system has been markedly centralized since the mid-sixties but the pace towards centralization of power got considerably accelerated since 60's. During that period political leadership and the state governments were being made subsequent to the central government. This exactly is not the climate under which Panchayati Raj can grow and flourish. Fourthly, the technology discovered at this time served only to reinforce the already powerful centralized pressures, in the process, relegating Panchayati Raj to a lower, even unimportant status.[25]

The third phase in the history of P.R. is the period between 1969-1983. This was a period of decline. No sincere or serious effort was made neither at the centre nor at the state level like the period of stagnation as mentioned above. On the political side, this phase witnessed the change of the Congress government at the centre and it culminated in the appointment of Ashok Mehta Committee in 1977 to revamp the P.R. structure. As far as the states were concerned, Karnataka, West Bengal and Andhra Pradesh made appreciable efforts to regenerate the P.R. structure in their areas.[26]

The Ashok Mehta Committee submitted its report in August 1978 and made 132 recommendations. Some of the important recommendations are:[27]

1. There should be a two-tier setup in the P.R. structure, i.e. a district level Zila Parishad and a Mandal Panchayat covering a population of 15,000 to 20,000.

2. The Committee suggested abolition of blocks as a development unit and emphasized that all development activities relating to district being performed by the state government should be placed under Zila Parishad.
3. The term of P.R.Is' should be four years and direct elections to these institutions should be held simultaneously.
4. Political parties can participate in the P.R. elections.
5. Nyaya Panchayat should be kept separate from the Development Panchayat and the former should be headed by a qualified judge.
6. P.R. bodies should normally not be superseded but if supersession becomes necessary elections should be held within 6 months.
7. Representation of the scheduled castes and scheduled tribes in all Panchayat bodies should be on the basis of their population.
8. There should be complete transfer of land revenue collections to P.R.Is. over a period of five years.
9. A permanent annual grant of not less than Rs. 2.50 per capita should be made to the Mandal Panchayats.
10. The Committee agreed to the need for some provisions in the Constitution in order to provide the P.R.Is. the requisite status as well as assurance of continuous functioning and wanted that this aspect should be considered.
11. All development functions relating to a district, which are now performed by the state government, should be placed under Zila Parishad.

Shri E.M.S. Nambodiripad, who was a member of the Committee, appended a note to the report in which he has expressed his views. Some of the important points are:

1. I am opposed to the suggestion of including the nominee of district level cooperative federation and

other categories of members of Zila Parishad and other P.R.Is. I am for purely elected bodies at all levels of P.R. bodies.

2. With regard to the election to all P.R.Is. proportional representation with the list system should be adopted.
3. I oppose the recommendation in favour of a qualified judge to preside over an elected Nyaya Panchayat being associated with him. The report itself admits that there is no enthusiasm for Nyaya Panchayat being associated with him. The Report itself admits that there is no enthusiasm for Nyaya Panchayat, the reasons being that people do not expect elected punches to be objective and do justice to the poor. Any proposal for bringing the judiciary closer to the people, can therefore, be considered only as a matter of reforming the judicial system and not as a part of democratic decentralization of administration. The government may consider the various reports, referred to in our report separately and not as part of strengthening P.R.Is.

Ashok Mehta Report has made an attempt to revitalize the P.R. system as established according to the reconsiderations of Balwantrai Mehta Report. The second Mehta has built his concept upon the first one, though in a certain way, he has given much of his own in the form of according constitutional status to P.R.Is. Thus, the two Mehtas constitute two landmarks in the history of local self-government in our country, though each has its distinctive conceptual framework of analysis and examination.

After the submission of Ashok Mehta Report—the phase of decline witnessed three more developments, that is,

THE CHIEF MINISTER'S CONFERENCE, 1979

It considered important recommendations of the Ashok Mehta Committee but it did not accept the concept of Mandal

Panchayats and favoured continuance of existing three-tier system.

WORKING GROUPS ON BLOCK AND DISTRICT PLANNING

In the beginning of 80's, a number of anti-poverty programmes were introduced for the implementation of which district rural development agencies and other related organizations of lower levels were created. Various aspects of decentralized planning were examined by two expert groups, namely, the Working group on Block Level Planning headed by M.L. Dantwala, 1977 and the Working Group on District Planning headed by C.H. Hanumantha Rao, 1983. Both groups recommended that the basic decentralized planning function has to be done at the district level.

THE PHASE OF REVIVAL (1983 ONWARDS)

After 1983, Panchayati Raj Institutions entered into an era of progress and prosperity. After Rajiv Gandhi came to power, he made sincere and whole-hearted efforts to implement the P.R. in letter and spirit. The scheme of P.R. as unfolded by the then Prime Minister, was the most comprehensive and radical blue print of participatory democracy officially published so far. Mr. Gandhi showed the necessary stamina.

L.M. SINGHVI COMMITTEE

In 1986, appeared the L. M. Singhvi Committee Report submitted at the insistence of the Ministry of Rural Development. After tracing the growth and development of democratic decentralization, the Singhvi Committee resurrected the nearly forgotten Gram Sabha, comprising all the inhabitants of a village and called it as the embodiment of direct democracy.[28]

SARKARIA COMMISSION

The Sarkaria Commission on Centre-State Relations (1988) did not favour the L.M. Singhvi Committee's to confer constitutional status to the P.R.Is.. The idea Commission advocated that the power of enacting any law on the Panchayats vests exclusively with states. Uniformity in these aspects of law throughout the territory of India is essential. The uniformity can be secured by adopting any of the alternatives from the following order of preference any of the alternatives

(i) By law, with respect to this matter, made by all the state legislatives in accordance with a model bill prepared on the basis of consensus at the forum of Inter-state council, recommended by us to be established under Article 263.

(ii) By a law, on this subject made by Parliament under Article 252 (i) with the consent of the legislatives of all the states.

(iii) By a parliamentary law, uniformly applicable throughout India containing provisions analogous to Articles 172 and 174 of the Constitution.

CONSTITUTIONAL STATUS

After independence, efforts were made by the states to introduce Panchayati Raj System. To give a boost to the system and to ensure its effective functioning, it became necessary to amend the Constitution. The Constitution (73rd Amendment (Act, 1992) that came into effect from 24th April, 1993 conferred constitutional status to Panchayats and government from the village upwards. It was considered by the experts that there is an imperative need to enshrine in the Constitution certain basic and essential features of P.R.I. to impart certainty, continuity and strength.

This Act has ushered a new era in the history of Indian

women has given them a chance to wield a greater power. It has a provision for not less than one-third of the elected members being women and not less than one-third chairpersons at the different tiers of Panchayat (that is village, block and zila) being women. This meant that about 20 lakh women would be contesting elections out of which about 8 lakh women would be elected as members and out of which 80,000 would be chairpersons.

THE PRESENT STATUS

Throughout the world women by virtue of gender, experience discrimination in terms of denial of equal access to power structure that controls societies and determines development issues and peace initiative. Further, the United Nations Report on women has pointed out that women perform two-thirds of world's work, receive only 10 per cent of the world's income and own only one per cent of the means of production.[29]

BRINGING IN POWER EQUATION

Power equation can be brought about only by change in societal conditions and an attitudinal change in women and men. This undoubtedly can become a reality in the P.R. system. The 29 subjects assigned under the eleventh schedule to the P.R.Is. are as follows:

1. Agriculture including agriculture extension.
2. Land improvements, land reforms, soil conservation.
3. Minor irrigation and watershed development.
4. Animal husbandry, dairying and poultry.
5. Fisheries
6. Social forest and farm forestry.
7. Minor forest produce.
8. Small scale industries including food processing industries.

9. Khadi, village and cottage industries.
10. Rural housing
11. Drinking water.
12. Fuel and fodder.
13. Roads, culverts, bridges, ferries and waterways.
14. Rural electrification including distribution of electricity.
15. Non-conventional energy resources.
16. Poverty alleviation programmes—I.R.D.P., J.R.Y.
17. Education including primary and secondary schools.
18. Technical training and vocational education.
19. Adult and non-formal education.
20. Libraries.
21. Cultural activities.
22. Markets and fairs
23. Health and sanitation including primary health centres and dispensaries.
24. Family welfare.
25. Women and child development.
26. Social welfare including welfare of handicapped and mentally retarded.
27. Welfare of weaker sections and in particular S.Cs. and S.Ts.
28. Public distribution system.
29. Maintenance of community assets.

Reservation of seats in the local body institutions for the women in all positions as per the provisions of 73rd and 74th Amendments to the Constitution of India, no doubt, is going to create a metamorphosis in the activities of women in polity, economy and society in the years to come. The initial apprehension and doubts over the readiness of women to come into power centres and to take up responsibilities of administering development on their own have been dispelled by their participation in the electoral process of the local body institutions in the month of October, 1996.

The elected leaders of the local bodies in Tamil Nadu while functioning in their respective domain, found problems like lack of training which was eventually given by the state. The effective functioning of the leaders fully relies on the leadership qualities of elected representatives. The elected women representatives who have stepped into the portals of power essentially need leadership training. Hence, a programme was conceived to offer leadership training to elected women of urban local bodies.[30] The training programme's content was a detailed discussion on the background of the 74th Constitutional Amendment Act and the role of women in administering development in their areas. Studies, carried out by the Institute of Social Science between 1987 and 1990, in Karnataka and another in 1991, in Kerala have shown that women did take part in large measures in P.R.Is. In Kerala, they have fought non-reserved constituencies for women.[31]

P.R.I. STATUS IN HIMACHAL PRADESH

BACKGROUND

P.R. system in H.P. was established in a statutory form under the provisions of the H.P. P.R. Act, 1952 in the year 1954. Only 280 Gram Panchayats existed prior to the enactment of the H.P. P.R. Act, 1952. However, after the enactment of the said Act, 466 Gram Panchayats were established in the year 1954 and the number of Gram Panchayats was increased to 638 during the year 1954 and the number of Gram Panchayats rose to 1695. In the merged area, a three-tier P.R. system was in existence under the provisions of Punjab, Panchayat Samiti and Zila Parishad Act, whereas two-tier system was prevalent in the state. With a view to bring uniformity in the P.R. system of the old and the newly merged areas, the H.P. P.R. Act, 1968 was enacted on 15th November, 1970. Besides this, the Nyaya Panchayats were also in existence in this state for discharging judicial functions but during the year 1977 the Nyaya Panchayats were abolished and the judicial functions were transferred to the Gram Panchayats. After the enactment of the said Act in the year 1970, the existing Gram Sabhas were reorganized/bifurcated from time to time and new Gram Sabhas/Gram Panchayats were established. At present, there are 3,087 Gram Sabhas, 75 Panchayat Samitis and 12 Zila Parishads constituted in the state. Detailed information about the number of the three-tiers is given later in Chapter 3.

Elections to establish three-tier Panchayati Raj system under the provision of 73rd Constitutional Amendment Act and the Himachal Pradesh Panchayati Raj Act, 1994 were held during December, 1995 except for the Panchayats of sub-division of Lahaul of district Lahaul Spiti, sub-division Pangi of district Chamba and four Gram Panchayats of district Kullu. The first meeting of the Panchayats at all the three levels was held on 23rd January, 1996 and as such the five years term of the elected representatives of Panchayats started with effect from 23rd January, 1996 which expired on 22nd January, 2001. Under the provisions of the Constitution and Panchayati Raj Act, it was mandatory to hold general elections to constitute new Panchayats before the expiry of the term of the representatives of P.R.Is. elected during December, 1995 and thus the general elections to the P.R.Is. were again held during December, 2000. As the term of the elected representatives of P.R.Is. in sub-division of Lahaul of district Lahaul Spiti, sub-division Pangi of district Chamba and four Gram Panchayats of district Kullu was to expire in June, 2001, therefore the elections in these areas were held on 5th and 7th June, 2001. The term of the present elected representatives has also started with effect from 23rd January, 2001 and in the case of sub-division of Lahaul of district Lahaul and Spiti, sub-division Pangi of district Chamba the term of office of representatives of P.R.Is. has started with effect from 24th June, 2001.[32]

With a view to restructure, rejuvenate and to give

constitutional status to the P.R.Is. the Constitution (73rd) Amendment Act, 1992 was enacted on 24th April, 1993. Essentially, the Amendment Act lays down certain ground rules which will constitute the basic structure or core features of the local authorities. This consists of a well defined duration, safeguards against external interference in the form of prolonged supresission, provision for regular elections of P.R. bodies, proper and meaningful representation of weaker sections and women and devolution of powers, authority and adequate finances to the Panchayats. The rest of the field has been left to the state government.

Himachal Pradesh is one of the states which has enacted the new legislation, that is, within one year from the date of the constitutional amendment. Simultaneously, the State Election Commission and the State Finance Commission was constituted by the government. The two-tier in the P.R. system, namely Gram Panchayat and Panchayat Samiti, which were already constituted in the state, gave way to the establishment of a three-tier P.R. system.

With a view to bring the state law relating to Panchayats in conformity with the provisions of the Panchayats (Extension to the Scheduled Areas) Act, 1996, the State Government has brought amendments in the Himachal Pradesh P.R. Act, 1994 vide the Himachal Pradesh Panchayati Raj (Second Amendment) Act, 1997.

REVIEW OF LITERATURE

The studies pertaining to Panchayati Raj, since its very inception has been the focus of attention of the policy makers, political leaders, administrators and researchers. A review of existing literature shows that various issues and problems, relating to Panchayati Raj have been discussed. Here, an attempt has been made to mention certain pioneering studies which have helped the author to understand the concepts, issues, problems and to develop acumen for the present study.

The important studies are mentioned as under:

Janet A. Flammang (1984) has discussed American politics at state and local levels and a revolution in women's electoral organisational and policy accompalishments. She inferenced that women are now transforming traditional political concepts but parties are still problematic for women. Also that, there is a significance in women's token status in government and majority status as voters.

N.J. Usha Rao in her book *Women in a Developing Society*, has discussed among other things about political awareness amongr rural women of *Chickmaglur*. The main objectives of the study was to know the interest displayed by the women voters in Chickmaglur in terms of their eagerness to know and willingness to spend time and efforts to give information regarding the elections. Another objective was to know political participation by way of attending political meetings and to know political awareness in terms of their or knowledge regarding the conditions contesting the election. It was found in this study that the urban elite conception of the rural illiterate women as irrational voters who blindly vote for women candidates or vote as ordered ny their menfolk is highly questionable. The women voters of Chickmaglur talukoin general seemed to bepolitically sensitive and well aware of the various issues confronting them. The high turnout of women for voting is perhaps some proof of their keen interest in voting, They involved themselves in politica meetings of different parties and discussed various issues.

The role of women in development has been discussed in a compilation, by Shanti Chakraborty of selected documents from International and Indian Archives 1975-1985. Here, it has been recommended that the national development policies should include the full integration of women in the development process as an integral part of general socio-economic progress, since this participation is an undeniably important index for fully determining the depth of development process. This should include the establishment and strengthening of machinery in the government as a co-ordination body to increase women's participation and access to developmental programmes. It also suggested promotion and support to organizations of women at the grass-root level and identification of the factors which restrict women's access to the rural infrastructure, means of production within their availability and by the promotion of grass-root organizations fo rural women.

Centre for Women's Development Studies, New Delhi, conducted a workshop for Middle Level Administrators and Grass Root Workdrs which was held at Bankura, West Bengal. Its main objectives were to look into the perceptions about the role, problems, potential and needs of poor rural women and to analyse the needs and ways to improve intra level communication and support to achieve the programme goals. Eighteen recommendstions were made in fields of training and applying for loans. It was also noted that women were totally neglected by corporaions and Boards set for them.

Satnam Kaur (1987) has discussed in her study that for integration rural women do, their contributions and potentials. She found out that respondents were paricipating in hundred per cent houdrhold chores. The level of participation of rueal women was highest in the health sector and lowest in agriculture programmes. She suggested that rural development based on growth and equires the full integration of women including euqal opportunities to develop land, employ their skills and equitable access to resources, inputs, services and organisation.

Sunita Pandey in her study, 'Women's Studies and Women's Movement' has shown the interdependence between the Women's and Women's Studies and the need for a closer collaboration between the two. Women's studies are being conducted in the Women's Studies Centres sponsored by University Grants Commission. Today, there are signs of the spirit of Women's Studies getting institutionalized within the very system. It is fighting against excessive academisation of women's movement that can lead to dilution of movement. For this subjective concern about the oppressed, women studies must be combined with scientific rigor and dispassionate analysis.

Surat Singh, Rahim (1989) have discussed the traditional leadership before independence in the Indian villages, leadership in the wake of Panchayati Raj and present emerging leadership on the basis of analysis of the available literature. They identified three main components of leadership—the leader, the follower and the situation. Notwithstanding the usage of co-option, at the village level, as a weapon to consolidate strength by a few men, in cannot be denied that the P.R.Is. have made it possible for the weaker sections to get into the elective offices and set the pace of further development.

The Centre for Women's Developments Studies conducted a workshop on Panchayati Raj and Women in 24th August 1980 at New Delhi. Dr. Vina Mazumdar, Director, CWDS said that the real voice of the majority of women was not heard at any level and nominated women functioned ad draftees, not representatives. While admitting the necessity of expanding women's participation in Panchayati Raj Institutions, the workshop decided to focus on the constraints and problems that prevent women's participation from being effective, by making some recommendations addressed to State legislatures. The workshop recommended that 33 per cent should be held as minimum rather that maximum level of reservation of women. Women should be represented on various Standing Committees. Training should be concurrent with participation to improve the quality of women's participation in decision-making.

Manikayamba has discussed the problems of employed women in the rural areas. The factors responsible for her problems were analysed and its ipact on her occupational role was studied. It was found that employed women in rural areas suffer from the problems arising out of her familial, professional and rural situations. The impression gathered about the development programme for rural women folk is that it is not satisfactory. To make the programme a success, a study of cultural factors such as belief patterns habits, world-views, social valuees, attitudes and class structure of rural women needs to be undertaken by the social scientists.

Leela Kasturi in her paper has said that in is appropriate to remember what Gandhi said about women's role in society. He had great faith in the women of India in forbearance capacity for sacrifice, dedication to the family and steadfastness. Gandhi went even further that the 1931 Congress declaration on Fundamental Rights in viewing political and legal aspects, equality for women as only the beginning. Women must have votes and an equal status. But the problem does not end there. It only commences at the point where women begin to affect the political deliberations of the nation.

N.K. Bannerjee says that grass-root empowerment also needs to be viewed from the stand point of share of grassroot women in the women's movement. While there is little doubt that the vitality of the Indian women's movement owes a great deal to the pressures generated from the grassroots, it would be far more difficult to answer the question how far has the women's movement been able to carry the grassroots? To induct grassroot women as vocal and active participants in the women' movement, is th challenge.

Snehlata Panda (1996) in her study has pointed out that even in the predominantly traditional setting of the State there is a positive pattern of women's leadership role. She conducted a survey of 81 elected women functionaries of Panchayati Raj Institutions in Orissa. It was revealed that traditional social structure and cultureal milieu have little influence on the perception of the rural people to choose women as panchayat representatives. They have traits of leadership and capability. Their non-party background and responsibilities which they shared as panchayat reposentatives and the class from which they have come, indicate positive directions of change in rural leadership.

Shanta Kohli Chandra has pointed our in her study that there must be efforts to improve the position of Indian women economically. They need to be self reliant. She also reached the conclusion that there is an inverse relationship between household economic status and female labour force. This study was an effort to assess the situation of employment of women in the Govt. of india in thirteen ministries. It was found that women need better access to organizations and mobility within labour market.

Kumud Sharma, in her paper, 'Power Vs Representation' has talked about 33 per cent representation of women in Panchayati Raj Insitutions and Lok Sabha. She has talked about issues with liberal democracy including the concepts of equality of opportuniy, merit and social justice. According to her, as as a socially and economically disadvantaged section, women have begun to understand the ways in which power is shared and why greater representation is needed to influence the redistribution of power and resources. The expectation of gains from representational policies definitely marks ad shift in the strategy of the women's movement.

Gowda and Dhadave have talked about relevance of political linkage in a democratic political system. This study covered 130 and 120 women leaders of Mandal Panchatats of the developed and backward taluka respectively of Karnataka State. It was found that statutory representation to rural women in Panchayati Raj Institutions has helped them signficantly to come out of the shackles to participate effectively in public life without diffidence and fear. The study showed that with the right type of orientation and opportunity, rural women could play a meaningful role in the political and development processes by way of influencing decision—making and also of getting development benefits to their villages through higher-level leaders. The empowerment of rural women has made their social and political development feasible.

Vina Mazumdar in her paper has revised its objectives so as to organise peasant women in centres of villages to increase their opportunities and capacities for collective and individual self employment through productive activities. The confidence of women at grassroot level can be increased by demonstration of their own collective abilities. Acquisition of knowledge and training that they need can be imparted by specialised government agencies and educational institutions. PRIs must be involved to achieve these aims.

The study of, 'Political Empowerment of Women: Case of Orissa PRIs' by Snehlata Panda emphasises on performance of women representatives in Panchayati Raj System based on 92 women candidates elected to Gram Sabha and Panchayat Samitis in Orissa. She covered significant factors like the respondents socio-enonomic and political background, factors contributing to their success in election and their political socialization and participation. She concluded that personal factors and interpersonal network were primary determiants for electing women. Women gained in status and commanded respect due to their effective performance as popular representatives.

It is evident from the above discussion that, a good number of studies have been carried out, dealing with different aspects of Panchayati Raj in India and women empowerment. In the present study, an attempt has been made to study the empowerment of women after 73rd Amendment on which nothing substantial has been studied. The present study is confined to the state of Himachal Pradesh where very little work has been carried out on the proposed topic. Hence, the present study makes it different from the above mentioned studies and is justified in the context of empowerment of women.

NOTES AND REFERENCES

1. M.R. Biju (1998), *Dynamics of New Panchayati Raj System*, Kanishka Publishers, New Delhi, p. 1.

2. S.L. Goel and Shalini Rajneesh (2003), *Panchayati Raj in India: Theory and Practice*, Deep and Deep Publications Pvt. Ltd., New Delhi, p. 3.
3. Seema Singh (2003), *Panchayati Raj and Women Empowerment*, Ocean Books Pvt. Ltd., New Delhi, p. 32
4. *Ibid.*, p. 33.
5. C. Rangrajan (2004), Chairman of the Finance Commission www.orissagov.nic.in/Panchayat/ fiscal.htm.
6. S.L. Goel and Shalini Rajneesh, *op. cit.*, p. 14.
7. Iqbal Narain (1970), *Panchayati Raj Administration of Controls and New Challenges*, The Indian Institute of Public Administration, New Delhi, pp. 3-4.
8. Speeches and Writings of Gopal Krishna Gokhale as quoted by A.K. Majumdar and Bhanwar Singh (1997), *Historical and Conceptual Development of Panchayati Raj*, Radha Publications, New Delhi, p. 59.
9. *Ibid.*, pp. 59-60.
10. S.N. Mishra and S.S. Singh (1993), *Roads to Model Panchayati Raj*, Mittal Publications, New Delhi, pp. 6-7.
11. S.K. Sharma and S.L. Malhotra (1977), *Integrated Rural Development—Approach Strategy and Perspectives*, Abhinav Publications, New Delhi, p. 23.
12. S.N. Mishra and S.S. Singh (1993), *op. cit.*, pp. 6-7.
13. S. Bhatnagar (1974), *Panchayati Raj in Kangra District*, Orient Longman, New Delhi, p. 17.
14. L.C. Jain et al. (1985), *Grass without Roads: Rural Government Under Government Auspices*, Sage Publications, New Delhi, p. 17.
15. S. Bhatnagar (1974), *op. cit.*, p. 17.
16. *Ibid.*, p. 5.
17. S.L. Goel and Shalini Rajneesh (2003), *op. cit.*, pp. 15-16.
18. Report of the Team for the Study of Community Projects and National Extension Service (1957), p. 6.
19. Balwantrai C. Mehta (1957), *op. cit.*, p. 6.
20. Government of India (1961), *Third Five-Year Plan*, Planning Commission, Delhi, p. 334.
21. M.R. Biju (1998), *op. cit.*, p. 26.
22. B. Maheshwari (1963), *Studies in Panchayati Raj*, Metropolitan, New Delhi, p. 11.
23. Sita Ram Singh (1986), "Revitalization of Panchayats", *Kurukshetra*, Vol. XXXIX, No. 6, New Delhi, p. 5.
24. Annual Report (1984-85), Department of Rural Development Quoted in Sita Ram Singh (1986), *op. cit.*, p. 5.
25. Report of the Central Council of Local Self-Government, Fifth

Meeting held at Hyderabad in 1959 as Quoted in M.R. Biju (1998), *op. cit.*, pp. 26-27.

26. *Ibid.*, p. 27.
27. *Ibid.*, pp. 27-28.
28. *Report of the Committee on Panchayati Raj Institutions (1998)*, Ministry of Agriculture and Irrigation, Development, Government of India, New Delhi (hereafter known as Asok Mehta Committee Report).
29. S.L. Goel and Shalini Rajneesh (2003), *op. cit.*, p. 19.
30. G. Palanithurai B.R. Dwaraki and S. Narayanaswamy (1997), *Major Issues in New Panchayati Raj System*, Kanishka Publishers, Delhi, p. 56.
31. *Ibid.*, p. 56.
32. Government of Himachal Pradesh (2004), *Annual Administrative Report,* Panchayati Raj Department, Shimla, p. 2.

2. OBJECTIVES AND METHODOLOGY

The focus of the study was to study the role of women leaders in Panchayati Raj in Himachal Pradesh. Most of the research work done so far on leadership in Panchayati Raj is in general and very little work has been done on empowerment of women in its political aspects, though the earlier studies were quite important as they provide the socio-economic and structural determinants for selecting the leadership at the village level. It is even more important to study about women leaders who have acquired power through the demographically elected bodies and who are actively involved in electing people's cooperation in the implementation of national plans related to socio-economic development since women leaders are working in a democratic framework and trying to engineer profound social and economic improvements through bringing new ideas and innovation for women.

As a field in an academic discipline, women studies owes its origins and existence to the distinctive practice of Women's Movement which gained momentum in the late 1960s and early 1970s. Women's studies have made women academically visible. However, if any substantial change in the position of women is to be brought about, then this academic visibility of women needs to be backed by political action.

Women leaders can better develop local schemes within the broad framework of national policies so that the people at the village level can be involved in the programme of development and brought into the mainstream of national policies.

The study of women leadership at the local level also carries a great political relevance since it may throw light on the essential conditions of democratic functioning of the grassroot democracies and the continuous inflow of new social success in achieving equality and highlight new catchment areas of leadership. One of the basic aims of Panchayati Raj had been to involve local people so that this study would help to locate and identify the impact of Panchayati Raj bodies on the recruitment of women leaders.

OBJECTIVES OF THE STUDY

The present study has been initiated with a view to examine the issues related to empowerment of women in P.R.Is. in Himachal Pradesh. The objectives of the study were:

1. to study the emergence and growth of P.R.Is,
2. to analyze the organizational structure of P.R.Is,
3. to analyze the educational, socio-economic, political and organizational background possessed by the women leaders of Panchayati Raj in Himachal Pradesh,
4. to look into the existing mode of relationship between the Executive and Women leaders,
5. to evaluate the role of women leaders in making the P.R.Is. programmes a success,
6. to critically evaluate the factors impeding better performance of women leaders and
7. to suggest measures to strengthen Panchayati Raj Institutions.

HYPOTHESIS

During the course of study, the following major hypothesis that the women leaders have failed to perform their duties at the grassroot level has been tested. It was further divided into sub-hypotheses:

(i) Low literacy and lack of knowledge amongst women leaders have resulted in non-performance of their role.

(ii) The negligence and indifferent attitude of executives towards women leaders have resulted in dissatisfaction amongst them.

METHODOLOGY

In order to achieve the above-mentioned objectives of the present study both primary and secondary data have been used. Secondary data pertaining to P.R.Is. and women leaders have been compiled from the related books, journals and various administrative reports of the State Government and the Department. For the collection of the primary data, a questionnaire-cum-interview schedule was administered to the respondents selected through sampling method.

SAMPLING METHOD

There were 2922 number of Gram Panchayats in Himachal Pradesh as on 10th March, 1999, 71 Panchayat Samitis and 12 Zila Parishads in Himachal Pradesh. From the office record of Department of Himachal Pradesh, it has been observed that district Kangra has highest number of Gram Panchayats, that is, 708, and 13 Panchayat Samitis besides one Zila Parishad (for details, see Table 2.1 and Table 2.2).

On the basis of the maximum number of Gram Panchayats, the district Kangra was selected for the purpose of collecting the first hand information through questionnaire.

For this purpose, a sample of 150 respondents, which account for about 50 per cent of total number, was drawn on the basis of random sampling from amongst women representatives. It included women members from Zila Parishad and at the Panchayat Samiti level, 2 Panchayat Samitis namely Panchrukhi and Rait were selected on the basis of wards/constituencies. At the Gram Panchayat level, Panchrukhi and Rait were selected on the basis of maximum number of women representatives.

TABLE 2.1: P.R.Is. IN HIMACHAL PRADESH

District	*Gram Panchayats*	*Panchayat Samitis*	*Zila Parishad*
1. Solan	195	05	01
2. Mandi	382	10	01
3. Hamirpur	209	05	01
4. Bilaspur	130	03	01
5. Una	217	04	01
6. Shimla	316	09	01
7. Kangra	708	13	01
8. Kinnaur	62	03	01
9. Lahaul-Spiti	41	02	01
10. Kullu	181	05	01
11. Sirmour	217	06	01
12. Chamba	264	07	01
Total	2922	72	12

Source: Compiled from office records of Panchayati Raj Directorate, Shimla.

TABLE 2.2: NUMBER OF WOMEN LEADERS IN P.R.Is. IN HIMACHAL PRADESH

District	*Gram Panchayats*	*Zila Parishad*	*Panchayat Samitis*
1. Solan	502	06	39
2. Mandi	826	12	81
3. Hamirpur	409	06	40
4. Bilaspur	304	05	31
5. Una	495	06	40
6. Shimla	620	08	60
7. Kangra	1311	19	125
8. Kinnaur	127	03	15
9. Lahaul-Spiti	71	03	08
10. Kullu	346	04	33
11. Sirmour	460	06	40
12. Chamba	542	06	46
Total	6013	84	558

Source: Ibid.

3. ORGANIZATIONAL STRUCTURE OF PANCHAYATI RAJ INSTITUTIONS IN HIMACHAL PRADESH

Our society is an organizational society. We are born in organizations, educated by organizations and most of us spend much of our lives working for organizations. We spend much of our leisure time paying, playing and praying in organizations. Most of us will die in an organization and when the time comes for burial, the largest organization of all, the state—must grant official permission.[1]

Sound organizational structure is an essential key for the success of an enterprise. Organization is a systematic bringing together of interdependent parts to form a unified whole through which authority, coordination and control may be exercised to achieve a given purpose.[2] Organizations can be defined as social units (or human groupings) deliberately constructed and reconstructed to seek specific goals.[3]

Here, a distinction between formal and informal organizations is relevant. The search for greater efficiency and effectiveness in organizations gave rise to the Classical Theory of Administration, perhaps more appropriately called Scientific Management, since the latter title expresses the emphasis of this organizational approach. Workers were seen as motivated by economic rewards and the organization characterized by a clearly defined division of labour with a highly specialized personnel and by a distinct hierarchy of authority. Out of this tradition comes the characterization of the formal organization as a blueprint according to which organizations are to be constructed and to which they ought to adhere.[4]

Arising in past as a reaction to scientific management, another school of thinking that gained prominence in the United States was the Human Relations—In contrast to Classical Theory, Human Relations emphasized the emotional, unplanned, non-rational elements in organizational behaviour. It discovered the significance of friendship and social groupings of workers for the organization. It also pointed out the importance of leadership in the organization and of emotional communication and participation. From these observations, the concept of informal organization was developed. This is sometimes viewed as what there is to organization beyond the formal structure, sometimes, as what the organizational life is really like as distinct from blueprint and charts.[5] The aim of this chapter is to evaluate the organizational setup of P.R.Is. in Himachal Pradesh.

The Himachal Pradesh Panchayati Raj Act, 1994 was enacted by the Himachal Pradesh Government and was made operative with effect from 23rd April, 1994. This Act has been further amended many times so far. The Himachal Pradesh Panchayati Raj Act, 1994 has been divided into XIV chapters and contains 200 sections. Five schedules have also been added to the Act. The main features of the Act as amended from time to time is discussed hereafter. The structure of P.R. in Himachal Pradesh according to the Act provides for four types of rural institutions, that is, Gram Sabha, Gram Panchayat, Panchayat Samiti and Zila Parishad which are to be constituted at the village level, block level and district level throughout the state.

GRAM SABHA

Gram Sabha which forms the core of the democratic decentralizations, needs to be given utmost attention. Thus the government has already taken steps to strengthen the institution of Gram Sabha. There are 200 sections given in the

Himachal Pradesh Panchayati Raj Act, 1994. The main features of this Act are:

SECTION 3: DECLARATION OF SABHA AREA

1. The government may, by notification, declare any village or group of contiguous villages with a population of not less than one thousand and not more than five thousand to constitute one or more Sabha areas for the purposes of this Act and also specify its headquarter, provided that in a scheduled area the government may by order declare any village or group of contiguous village with a population of less than one thousand to constitute a Sabha area:

   Provided further that the government may after having due regard of the geographical location, lack of means of transport and communication and administrative convenience, declare an area comprising a village or group of contiguous villages a population either less than one thousand or more than five thousand to constitute a Sabha area;
2. The government may, at the request of the Gram Sabha concerned or otherwise and after previous proposal by a notification, at a notification, at any time;
   (a) Increase any Sabha area by including within such Sabha area any village or group of villages, or
   (b) Diminish any Sabha area by excluding from such Sabha area any village or group of villages; or
   (c) Alter the headquarter of any Sabha area or
   (d) Alter the name of any Sabha area; or
   (e) Declare that any area shall cease to be a Sabha area:
3. If the whole of the Sabha area is included in a municipality the Sabha area shall cease to exist and its assets and liabilities shall in the manner prescribed be disposed of.

SECTION 4: ESTABLISHMENT OF GRAM SABHA

(1) The government may, by order, establish a Gram Sabha by name in every Sabha area.

   (1) For every Gram Sabha established under subsection (1), there shall be a list of voters which shall be prepared in accordance with the provision of this act and the rules made thereunder.

   (2) Every person who is qualified to be registered in the legislative assembly roll relatable to the Sabha area or whose name is entered therein and is ordinarily resident within the Gram Sabha area shall be entitled to be registered in the list of voters of that Sabha provided that no person shall be entitled to be registered in the list of voters for more than one Sabha area.

Meeting and Quorum of the Sabha

(1) Every Sabha shall hold four general meetings in each year and every meeting shall be held on the first Sunday of January, April, July and October and it shall be the responsibility of the Pradhan to convene such meetings. Provided further that the pradhan may, at any time or upon a requisition in writing of not less than one-fifth members of the Gram Sabha or if required by the Panchayat Samiti, Zila Parishad or the Deputy Commissioner, shall, within 30 days from the receipt of such requisition hold an extraordinary general meeting, provided further that where a Pradhan fails to convene the meetings under this sub-section, the prescribed authority shall convene such meetings within a period of thirty days.

(2) The time and place of all the meetings of the Gram Sabha shall be published in the prescribed manner.

(3) For any general meeting of the Gram Sabha, representation of at least one-third of the total number of

families represented by one or more members of the Gram Sabha shall form a quorum and decisions will be taken by a majority of members present and voting :

Provided that for a meeting adjourned for want of quorum, at least one-fifth of the total number of family's representation of at least one-fifth of the total number of families represented by one or more members of the Gram Sabha shall be required for holding the adjourned meeting.

SECTION 6: DEFECT OR OMISSION IN ENROLMENT OF MEMBERS NOT TO VITIATE ACT OR PROCEEDINGS OF THE GRAM SABHA

No defect or omission in the enrolment of a member shall vitiate any act or proceeding of a Gram Sabha not less than two-thirds of the members at the time, the act is done, or the proceedings are taken, were duly qualified members thereof.

SECTION 7: FUNCTIONS OF GRAM SABHA

(1) The Gram Sabha shall perform the following functions namely;

(a) Mobilize voluntary labour and contribution in kind and cash for the community welfare programmes;

(b) Identification of beneficiaries for the implementation of developmental schemes pertaining to the village;

(c) Rendering assistance in the implementation of developmental schemes pertaining to the village;

(d) Promotion of unity and harmony among all sections of society in the Sabha area;

(e) Seek clarifications from the Pradhan, Up-Pradhan and members of the Gram Panchayat about any particular activity, scheme, income and expenditure and

(f) Such other matters as may be prescribed.

(2) The Gram Sabha shall consider the following matters and make recommendations and suggestions to the Gram Panchayat namely;

(a) The annual statement of accounts of the Gram Panchayat, the report of the administration of the preceding financial year and the last audit note and replies, if any, made thereto;

(b) The report in respect of development programmes of the Gram Panchayat relating to the preceding year and development programmes proposed to be undertaken during the current year.

(c) The promotion of unity and harmony among all sections of society in the village;

(d) The programme of adult education within the village;

(e) Any other matter which the Panchayat Samiti, Zila Parishad, the Deputy Commissioner or any other officer authorized in this behalf may require to be placed before the Gram Sabha, and

(f) Such other matters as may be prescribed.

(g) The Gram Panchayat shall give due consideration to the recommendations and suggestions of the Gram Sabha.

(3) The Gram Sahba may also form one or more vigilance committee(s) consisting of not less than five persons, who are not members of the Gram Panchayat to supervise the Gram Panchayat works, schemes and other activities and to put up reports concerning them in its meeting and shall also send a copy of the said report to such an authority as may be prescribed for this purpose.

SECTION 7-A: CONSTITUTION OF THE UP-GRAM SABHA

There shall be a Up-Gram Sabha for each ward of a Gram

Sabha:

(i) All members of the Gram Sabha residing within the area of the ward shall be members of the Up-Gram Sabha

(ii) Every Up-Gram Sabha shall hold two general meetings in each year and it shall be the responsibility of the member of the Gram Panchayat representing the ward to convene such meetings. The meetings of the Up-Gram Sabha shall be presided over by the member of the Gram Panchayat, representing the ward, who shall also record the proceedings.

(iii) The time and place of the meetings of the Up-Gram Sabha shall be fixed and notified by the member of the Gram Panchayat representing the ward.

(iv) The Up-Gram Sabha shall nominate its members to represent it in the general meeting of the Gram Sabha from attending the general meetings of the Gram Sabha.

(v) The Up-Gram Sabha may deliberate on issues relating to its area and make recommendations to the Gram Panchayat or Gram Sabha.

GRAM PANCHAYATS

SECTION 8: CONSTITUTION OF GRAM PANCHAYATS

(1) There shall be a Gram Panchayat for a Gram Sabha and every Gram Sabha shall, in the prescribed manner, elect from amongst its members a Pradhan and Up-Pradhan of the Sabha who shall also be called the Pradhan and Up-Pradhan of the Gram Panchayat and shall also elect from amongst its members and executive committee called the Gram Panchayat consisting of such number or persons not being less than seven and more than fifteen, including Pradhan and Up-Pradhan, as the government may by

notification determine:

Provided that the number of members, excluding Pradhan and Up-Pradhan to be assigned to each Gram Sabha shall be determined on the following scale:

(a) With a population not exceeding 1750 ... 5
(b) With a population exceeding 1750 but not exceeding 2750 ... 7
(c) With a population exceeding 2750 but not exceeding 3750 ... 9
(d) With a population exceeding 3750 but not exceeding 4750 ... 11
(e) With a population exceeding 4750 ... 13

Provided further that the number of members of a Gram Panchayat, excluding Pradhan and Up-Pradhan, shall be determined in such a manner that the ratio between the population of the Gram Sabha and the number of seats of members in such a Panchayat to be filled by election shall, so far as practicable, be the same throughout the Sabha area.

(2) Seats shall be reserved in a Gram Panchayat
(a) for the scheduled castes and
(b) for the scheduled tribes.

And the number of seats so reserved shall bear as nearly as may by same proportion to the total number of seats in the Gram Panchayat as the scheduled tribes in the Sabha area bears to the total population of the Sabha area; provided that in case no reservation of seats is possible as aforesaid due to small population of the scheduled castes and the population of scheduled castes of the Sabha area is at least five per cent of the total population of the Sabha areas, one seat shall be reserved for the scheduled castes in such a Gram Panchayat. Provided further that where there is no eligible candidate belonging to the scheduled castes to be elected as a member of the Gram Panchayat, no seat shall be reserved for scheduled castes.

Provided further that in non-tribal areas where there is scheduled tribes population in a Gram Sabha, seats shall be reserved for such members of the scheduled tribes within the reservation provided for the members of the scheduled castes and the determination of seats to be reserved amongst the scheduled castes and scheduled tribes shall be in proportion to their population in that Gram Sabha.

Provided further that the member of the Panchayat Samiti, representing a part of whole of the Gram Sabha area shall also be the member of the concerned Gram Panchayat(s) and shall have the right to vote.

(3) Not less than one-third of the total number of seats reserved under sub-section (2) shall be reserved for women belonging to the scheduled castes or as the case may be, the scheduled tribes.

(3-A) Not less than one-third (including the number of seats reserved for women belonging to the scheduled castes and scheduled tribes) of the total number of seats to be filled by direct election in every Gram Panchayat shall be reserved for women.

(4) The state government may, by general or special order, reserve such number of seats for persons belonging to backward classes in a Gram Panchayat, not exceeding the proportion to the total number of seats to be filled by direct election in the Gram Panchayat as the population of the persons belonging to backward classes in that Gram Sabha area bears to the total population of that area and may further reserve not less than one-third of the total seats reserved under this sub-section for women belonging

to backward classes.

(5) The seats reserved under sub-sections (2), (3), (3-A) and (4) shall be allotted by rotation to different constituencies in the Sabha area in such manner as may be prescribed.

(6) If for any reason the election to any Gram Panchayat does not result in the election of required number of persons as specified in sub-section (i), the Deputy Commissioner, shall within one month from the date on which the names of the elected persons are published by him under section 126 arrange another election to make up the deficiency.

Section 9: Meetings of Gram Panchayat

The meeting of the Gram Panchayat shall be public.

Section 10: Maintenance of Gram Panchayat records etc.

The secretary of the Gram Panchayat, under the overall supervision of the Pradhan and in his absence under the supervision of the Up-Pradhan shall be responsible for the custody and maintenance of all prescribed records and registers and other property belonging to or vested in the Gram Sabha or the Gram Panchayat.

Section 11: Functions of Gram Panchayat

(1) It shall be the duty of a Gram Panchayat in so far as the Gram Panchayat funds allow to perform specified in Schedule I.

(2) Notwithstanding anything contained in this put the state government may, by general or specific order, entrust to the Gram Panchayat preparation of plans and implementation of schemes for economic development and social justice specified in Schedule II.

(3) The state government may, by general or special

order, add to any of the functions of the Gram Panchayat or withdraw the functions and duties entrusted to such a Gram Panchayat, when the state government undertakes the execution of any of the functions entrusted to the Gram Panchayat, the Gram Panchayat shall not be responsible for such functions so long as the state government does not re-entrust such functions to the Gram Panchayat.

(4) The government may, by notification and subject to such conditions as may be specified therein:

(a) Transfer to any Gram Panchayat the management and maintenance of a forest situated in the Gram Sabha area;

(b) Make-over to the Gram Panchayat the management of waste lands, pasture lands, or vacant lands belonging to the government situated within the Gram Sabha area;

(c) Transfer to the Gram Panchayat the production of any irrigation work and its execution and the regulation/distribution of water from any such work;

(d) Transfer to the Gram Panchayat any public property situated within the jurisdiction of the Gram Sabha;

(e) Entrust the Gram Panchayat with the collection of land revenue on behalf of the government and the maintenance of such records on behalf of the government as are connected therewith and

(f) Entrust such other functions as may be prescribed.

Provided that when any transfer of the management and maintenance of a forest is made under clause (a) or the transfer of any irrigation work is made under clause (c), the government shall direct that any amount required for such management and maintenance or an adequate portion of the income from such forest or irrigation work be placed at the disposal of the Gram Panchayat.

(5) A Gram Panchayat shall have powers to do all acts necessary for or incidental to carry out the functions entrusted assigned or delegated to it, and, in particular and without prejudice to the foregoing powers to exercise all powers specified under this Act.

SECTION 12

Power of removal of encouragements and nuisance have been given in this section.

SECTION 13

Power to make general orders.

SECTION 15

Penalty for disobedience of a special or general order to the Panchayat.

SECTION 16

Power to enquire and make report about misconduct of certain officials.

SECTION 17

Power to contract for the collection of taxes and other dues.

SECTION 18

Power to introduce prohibition is given.

SECTION 19

Constitution and functions of standing committees is given.

SECTION 20

Joint Committees.

SECTION 21

Work to be entrusted to Joint Committee.

PANCHAYAT SAMITI

SECTION 77: ESTABLISHMENT OF PANCHAYAT SAMITI

(1) For each block, there shall be a Panchayat Samiti having jurisdiction over the entire block excluding such portions of the block as are included in a municipality constituted under any law for the time being in force.

(2) If after a Panchayat Samiti, is constituted for a block under sub-section (i), the block is redelimited, the government shall reconstitute a Panchayat Samiti for the redelimited block under the provision of that sub-section. Provided that the redelimitation of any block under the subsection shall not have the effect till the expiration of the term of the elected members of the existing Panchayat Samiti.

SECTION 78: CONSTITUTION OF PANCHAYAT SAMITI

(1) Every Panchayat Samiti shall consist of:

  (a) the directly elected members from territorial constituencies as determined under the act;

  (b) the members of the house of the people and the members of the legislative assembly of the state representing constituencies which comprise wholly or partly the Panchayat Samiti area;

  (c) the members of the council of states, where they are registered as electors within the Panchayat Samiti area;

  (d) one-fifth of the Pradhans of Gram Panchayats in the Panchayat Samiti area, by rotation, for such period as the prescribed authority may determine, by lot:

Provided that a Pradhan who was a member under this clause for one term shall not be eligible to become member for a second term during the remainder of his term of office as Pradhan.

(2) The Pradhans of Gram Panchayat and other members of the Panchayat Samiti, whether or not chosen by direct election from territorial constituencies in the Panchayat Samiti, shall have the right to vote in the meetings of the Panchayat Samiti. In the election and removal of the chairman or vice-chairman only the elected members shall have the right to vote.

(3) The number of elected members of a Panchayat Samiti under clause (a) of sub-section (1) shall consist of persons elected from the territorial constituencies in the Samiti areas as may be notified from time to time by the government at the rate of one member for every three thousand five hundred population or part there of:

Provided that in a Panchayat Samiti area having a population of not exceeding fifty-two thousand five hundred there shall be minimum of 15 elected members. Provided further that where the population of a Panchayat Samiti area is more than one lakh and forty thousand it shall be divided into territorial constituencies in such manner that the total number of constituencies shall not exceed forty and the population of each constituency shall as far as practicable, be the same in each constituency.

Provided further that the government may irrespective of the population of the Panchayat Samiti area, declare, by a notification that the provisions of this section shall apply to a Panchayat Samiti in a scheduled area, subject to such exceptions and modifications as may be specified by it in such a notification.

(4) Seats shall be reserved in a Panchayat Samiti for the:

(a) Scheduled Castes and
(b) The Scheduled Tribes

and the number of seats so reserved shall bear as nearly as may be, the same proportion to the total number of seats to be filled by direct election in that Panchayat Samiti as the population of the scheduled castes in that Panchayat Samiti area or the scheduled tribes in that Panchayat Samiti area bears to the total population of that area and such seats may be allotted by rotation to different constituencies in a Panchayat Samiti in such manner, as may be prescribed.

SECTION 79

It deals with the election of Chairman and Vice-Chairman of Panchayat Samiti.

SECTION 80

It deals with meetings held by Panchayat Samiti members.

A meeting of a Panchayat Samiti can be ordinary or special convened by the Chairman and in his absence by the Vice-Chairman.

SECTION 81

It deals with the functions of the Panchayat Samiti subject to the provision of this Act and the rules made thereunder and subject to general or special orders, as may be issued by the state government from time to time, So far as the Panchayat Samiti funds allow to make reasonable provision in the Samiti area for the following matters:

(a) Integrated Rural Development, Agriculture, Social Forestry, Animal Husbandry, etc.;
(b) Provision of emergency relief in cases of distress caused by fires, floods, drought, earthquake, scarcity, etc.;
(c) Arrangement in connection with local pilgrimage and

festivals;

(d) Management of public ferries;

(e) Management of public markets, public meals and exhibitions and

(f) Any other function with the approval of the state government or Zila Parishad.

SECTION 82

This section deals with the entrustment of certain functions of state government to a Panchayat Samiti.

SECTION 83

This section deals with the power of the state government in relation to functions of Panchayat Samiti.

SECTION 84

This section deals with the standing committees which are;

(a) General Standing Committee.

(b) Finance, Audit and Planning Committee.

(c) Social Justice Committee.

SECTION 85

This section deals with the functions of the standing committees relating to the establishment matters, communications buildings rural housing, village extension relief against natural calamities, water supply and all residuary matters.

SECTION 86

This section deals with the procedure of standing committees according to which the Panchayat Samiti may frame bylaws relating to election of members of committees, conduct of business therein and all other matters.

SECTION 87

It deals with consultative committees which may be appointed by the Panchayat Samiti for enquiry and report or for opinion on such special subjects relating to the purpose of this Act.

ZILA PARISHAD

SECTION 88

This section deals with establishment of Zila Parishad.

(1) For each district there shall be a Zila Parishad, having jurisdiction over the entire district excluding such portions of the district as are included in a municipality constituted under any law for the time being in force.

SECTION 89

This section deals with the constitution of Zila Parishad.

1. Every Zila Parishad shall consist of:
   (a) the directly elected members from territorial constituencies in the district as determined under this Act;
   (b) the members of the House of People and the members of the State Legislative Assembly representing a part or whole of the district whose constituencies lie within the district;
   (c) the members of the council of states, where they are registered as electors within the district, and
   (d) the Chairmen of all Panchayat Samitis in the district.

   Provided that when the total number of members under clauses (b), (c) and (d) exceed the total number of members under clause (a), only one-fifth of the members under clause (d) shall be selected by rotation for such period as the prescribed authority may determine, by lot. Subject to the condition that a chairman who was a member under this clause for one term shall not be eligible to become member for second term during the remainder of his term of office as the Chairman of Panchayat Samiti.

SECTION 90

It deals with the Election of the Chairman and Vice-Chairman within one week of declaration of the results by the Deputy Commissioner.

SECTION 91

This section deals with meetings of Zila Parishad:

(1) to be convened by the Chairman and in his absence Vice Chairman;

(2) a Zila Parishad shall ordinarily meet at its headquarters at least four times in each year for the transaction of its business and not more than three months shall be allowed to lapse between any two successive meetings.

SECTION 92

It deals with the functions of the Zila Parishad subject to the provisions of this Act and rules made thereunder, it shall be the duty of the Zila Parishad to:

(i) control, coordinate and guide, the Panchayat Samiti and Gram Panchayat within the district;

(ii) coordinate and consolidate the Panchayat Samiti plans;

(iii) coordinate the demands for grants for special purpose received from the Panchayat Samiti and forward them to the state government;

(iv) secure the execution of the plans, projects schemes or other works common to two or more Panchayat Samiti in the district;

(v) advise the state government in the developmental activities;

(vi) exercise and perform such other powers and functions as the state government may, confer on it.

SECTION 93

This section deals with the entrustment of certain functions of state government to a Zila Parishad as given below:

1. The state government may entrust to a Zila Parishad the functions in relation to any matter to which the executive authority of the state government exceeds or in respect of functions which have been entrusted to the state government by the central government, and the Zila Parishad shall be bound to perform such functions. It shall have necessary powers to perform such functions.
2. Where functions are entrusted to a Zila Parishad under sub-section (1) the Zila Parishad shall in the discharge of those functions act as an agent of the state government.
3. There shall be paid by the state government to the Zila Parishad such sum as may be deemed necessary for discharging the functions entrusted to it under this section.
4. The Zila Parishad shall for the purpose of discharging the functions entrusted to it under this section, be under the general control of the state government and shall comply with such directions as may from time to time, be given to it.

SECTION 94

It deals with the power of the state government in relation to functions of Zila Parishad.

(1) Notwithstanding anything contained in the Act the state government may by general or special order, entrust to the Zila Parishad for preparation for plans and implementation of schemes for economic

development and social justice including those in relation to the matters listed in Schedule-II.

(2) The state government may, by general or special order, add to any of the direction of the Zila Parishad or withdraw the function of the Zila Parishad or withdraw the function and duties entrusted to such a Zila Parishad, when the state government undertakes the execution of any of the functions entrusted to the Zila Parisha, the Zila Parishad shall not be responsible for such function so long as the state government does not re-entrust such functions to the Zila Parishad.

SECTION 95

This section deals with standing committees.

The Zila Parishad shall have the following standing committees, namely:

(a) General Committee;
(b) Final, Audit and Planning Committee;
(c) Social Justice Committee;
(d) Education and Health Committee and
(e) Agriculture and Industries Committee.

SUMMARY

Organisational structure of Panchayati Raj Institutions in Himachal Pradesh was studied in this chapter. According to the H.P. P.R. Act, 1994 enacted by the H.P. Government with effect from 23rd April, 1994, the main features found were quite enlightening.

- The government may declare any village or group of contiguous villages with a population of not less than one thousand and not more than five thousand to constitute one or more Sabha areas.
- The government may increase, diminish, alter the headquarter or the name or cease any Sabha area.

- Every Sabha shall hold four general meetings in each year.
- Functions of Gram Sabha included mobilization of voluntary labour and contribution in kind and cash for the community welfare programmes, identification of beneficiaries for the implementation of development schemes pertaining to the village, etc.
- There shall be an Up-Gram Sabha residing within the area of the ward having two general meetings in each year.
- Seats shall be reserved in a Gram Panchayat for the Scheduled Castes and Scheduled Tribes.
- For each block, there shall be a Panchayat Samiti consisting of directly elected members from territorial constituencies, members of the legislative assembly of the state, members of the council of states and one-fifth of the Pradhans of Gram Panchayats in the Panchayat Samiti area.
- For every district, there shall be a Zila Parishad consisting of directly elected members from territorial constituencies in the district, members of the House of People, members of the State Legislative Assembly, members of the council of states and the Chairmen of all Panchayat Samitis in the district.
- Functions of Zila Parishad include control and coordination of Panchayat Samiti plans, etc.

NOTES AND REFERENCES

1. Amitai Etzioni (1978), *Modern Orgamizations,* Prentice-Hall 08 India Pvt. Ltd., New Delhi., p. 1.
2. *Ibid.*, p. 3.
3. Talcott Pearsons (1960), *op. cit.*, p. 17.
4. Amitai Etzioni, *op. cit.*, p. 20.
5. *Ibid.*, p. 20
6. Government of Himachal Pradesh (1994), *Panchayati Raj Act*, Shimla, p. 4.

4. SOCIO-ECONOMIC BACKGROUND OF OFFICIALS AND MEMBERS OF P.R.Is.

The socio-economic development of any rural institution of administration depends on the quality of leadership to a large extent. The analysis of socio-cultural factors like age, caste, religion, occupation, income, education, etc. in relation to leadership in P.R.Is., implies that some of these factors are important for leadership.[1] A study of characteristics of Panchayat leadership is important for three reasons. Firstly, the performance of the Panchayat as a human group depends much upon the experience and attitude of the members upon which it must draw while it makes the decisions. Secondly, leadership development is a very important responsibility of the community development agency. The achievements in this respect can be verified by reference to the changing characteristics of Panchayat leadership. Thirdly, the functioning of the Panchayat as a democratic organization of the community depends upon the nature of the to and fro relationship between voters and the office bearer of Panchayat.[2]

Therefore the leadership of these village Panchayats plays a vital role in the successful implementation of various developmental programmes. If the leadership is change-prone dynamic, articulate and forward looking, it would go a long way in ushering in the desired change in the socio-economic life of rural India.[3] The present study is intended to cover the women rural leadership at grass-root level. The aim of the study was to investigate the socio-economic background of the Panchayat Samiti's leadership as well as the officials of the Panchayat Samiti; more especially to find out whether age, caste, education, land ownership, income, occupation and political affiliation have any impact on the pattern of leadership.

There are a number of characteristics of respondents which influence their role performance which is the subject matter of this study. Given below are the findings with respect to various indicators.

1. CASTE COMPOSITION

Caste plays an important role in traditional Panchayats as the traditionally dominant castes play a dominant role in the functioning of the traditional Panchayats. As a result of this, the leadership in traditional Panchayats is generally centred in the hands of elite castes but due to the introduction of statutory Panchayats and provision for the reservation of seats for scheduled castes, the complexion of Panchayats has emerged in recent years. Caste plays an important role in shaping the Panchayat leadership because the leadership is dominated by the elite castes.[4]

Table 4.1 reveals that out of the total sample population in Block Rait, only 4 per cent respondents belonged to the

TABLE 4.1: CASTE COMPOSITION

Caste	*Block Rait*		*Block Panchrukhi*	
	No. of Respondents	*Per-centage*	*No. of Respondents*	*Per-centage*
1. Brahmin	3	4.00	16	21.33
2. Kshatriya	15	20.00	20	26.67
3. Vaishya	50	66.67	14	18.67
4. Scheduled Caste	7.	9.33	25	33.33
5. Others	-	-	1	-
Total	75	100.00	75	100.00

Brahmin caste while in Block Panchrukhi 21.33 per cent respondents belonged to the Brahmin caste, women members belonging to Kshatriya caste in Block Rait were 20 per cent and 26.67 per cent respondents in Block Panchrukhi belonged to this caste. The third section of the society, that is, the Vaishyas, ruled the analysis. A majority of 66.67 per cent members of Block Rait and 18.67 per cent members of Block Panchrukhi belonged to the Vaishya caste. Lastly, in Block Rait, 9.33 per cent members and in Block Panchrukhi, 33.33 per cent members belonged to the scheduled caste. It became clear from the Table 4.1 that the women leadership was dominated by Vaishya community.

2. EDUCATION

In a developing democratic society, education plays an important role in shaping the leadership pattern.[5] For leaders in P.R.Is. it is much more important because if they have a sufficient level of education, they can better understand the objectives of P.R. and appreciate their role into the functioning.[6] Table 4.2 shows the education standard of officials.

It is revealed from the Table 4.2 that 16 per cent respondents were illiterate in Block Rait and only 1.33 per cent respondents were illiterate in Block Panchrukhi. 21.33

TABLE 4.2: EDUCATION

Qualification	*Block Rait*		*Block Panchrukhi*	
	Respondents	*Percentage*	*Respondents*	*Percentage*
1. Illiterate	12	16.00	1	1.33
2. Upto Primary	16	21.33	12	16.00
3. Upto Middle	20	26.67	19	25.33
4. Upto Matric	18	24.00	13	17.34
5. Upto +2	7	9.33	12	16.00
6. Above +2	2	2.67	18	24.00
Total	75	100.00	75	100.00

per cent Panchayat members had studied up to Primary in Block Rait while in Block Panchrukhi 16 per cent respondents had studied up to primary level. 26.67 per cent respondents were educated up to middle in Block Rait and 25.33 per cent respondents had studied up to middle in Block Panchrukhi 24 per cent members and 17.34 per cent members had studied up to matric in Block Rait and Block Panchrukhi respectively.

9.33 per cent members were educated up to +2 in Block Rait while 16 per cent members in Block Panchrukhi Only 2.67 per cent members had studied above +2 level in Block Rait while 24 per cent members in Block Panchrukhi were educated above +2.

So, the above analysis shows that majority of the members were matriculate i.e. literates out of 75 respondents in Block Rait. Similar was the position in Block Panchrukhi. However, 24 per cent were above +2. This ongoing analysis shows that the sample population was quite educated which is a good sign in the path of P.R.Is.

3. OCCUPATION

Occupation is important in determining the leadership structure. Persons of only those occupations can afford to be leaders who have free time and stay in the village. Only agriculturists, labourers and traditional occupation holders get the opportunity to stay in the village and among these groups, the agriculturist class gets more leisure than the other occupation groups.[7] The occupation of members of P.R.Is. is given in Table 4.3.

57.33 per cent respondents were engaged in agriculture in

TABLE 4.3: OCCUPATION

Occupation	*Block Rait*		*Block Panchrukhi*	
	Respondents	*Percentage*	*Respondents*	*Percentage*
1. Agriculture	43	57.33	48	64.00
2. Business	11	14.67	15	20.00
3. Others	21	28.00	12	16.00
Total	75	100.00	75	100.00

Block Rait while 64 per cent members in Block Panchrukhi. 14.67 per cent respondents were associated in business in Block Rait whereas 20 per cent members in Block Panchrukhi. 28 per cent respondents involved themselves in other activities in Block Rait while 16 per cent members in Block Panchrukhi. It can be concluded from the above analysis that majority of the respondents belonged to the category of agriculturists. This can be supported by the fact that the blocks to which the sample population belonged to were the agriculture sector.

4. INCOME

It was found that 53.34 per cent respondents were found to be in the category of annual income (including family) to be below Rs. 50,000 in Block Rait and 41.33 per cent members in

TABLE 4.4: INCOME

Annual Income	*Block Rait*		*Block Panchrukhi*	
	Respondents	*Percentage*	*Respondents*	*Percentage*
1. Below Rs. 50,000	40	53.34	31	41.33
2. Below 1,00,000	15	20.00	38	50.67
3. Below 2,00,000	10	13.33	5	6.67
4. Above 2,00,000	10	13.33	1	1.33
Total	75	100.00	75	100.00

Block Panchrukhi. 20 per cent respondents belonged to the income group of annual income below Rs. 1,00,000 in Block Rait and 50.67 per cent respondents in Block Panchrukhi. 13.33 per cent members were found in the income group of above Rs. 2,00,000 in Block Rait and only 1.33 per cent members were found to be earning above Rs. 2,00,000. It can be said according to the ongoing analysis that the majority of the members belonged to the lowest income group of annual income below Rs. 50, 000. This means that the majority of them belonged to the low income group.

5. SIZE OF FAMILY

Size of family is one of the determining factors in rural leadership especially women because it makes a difference how much time a woman may be able to devote to politics and developmental duties. Table 4.5 shows the importance of size of family. It shows that 86.67 per cent respondents the total sample population belonged to families having less than 5 members in Block Rait and 46.67 per cent respondents in Block Panchrukhi. 13.33 per cent respondents were found to be in the category of family having more than 5 members in Block Rait and 53.33 per cent members in Block Panchrukhi.

TABLE 4.5: SIZE OF FAMILY

Family members	*Block Rait*		*Block Panchrukhi*	
	Respondents	*Percentage*	*Respondents*	*Percentage*
1. Less than 5	65	86.67	35	46.67
2. More than 5	10	13.33	40	53.33
Total	75	100.00	75	100.00

One can say from this analysis that majority of the women members had a small family of having less than 5 members. This shows that the elected women P.R.Is. were socially aware and believed in a small number of children.

6. TIME SPENT IN HOUSEHOLD WORK

As our society trend goes, it is considered to be quite normal that a woman's primary job is to take care of her house and rest is all secondary. The rest includes the job or any social work which she plans to do. Table 4.6 reveals that 8 per cent respondents expressed that they spent more than 2 hours in household work in Block Rait while only 1.33 per cent respondents spent more than 2 hours in household work in

TABLE 4.6: TIME SPENT IN HOUSEHOLD WORK

Time Spent	Block Rait		Block Panchrukhi	
	Respondents	Percentage	Respondents	Percentage
1. More than 2 hours	6	8.00	1	1.33
2. More than 4 hours	25	33.33	6	8.00
3. More than 6 hours	30	40.00	37	49.33
4. More than 8 hours	14	18.67	31	41.34
Total	75	100.00	75	100.00

Block Panchrukhi. 33.33 per cent respondents admitted of spending more than 4 hours in household work in Block Rait and 8 per cent respondents in Block Panchrukhi.

There were 40 per cent respondents who said that they spent more than 6 hours in Block Rait and 49.33 per cent members in Block Panchrukhi. Finally, 18.67 per cent respondents expressed of spending more than 8 hours in household work in Block Rait and 41.34 per cent members in Block Panchrukhi. It becomes clear from the above analysis that majority of the members spent more than 6-8 hours in household work.

7. HELP FROM HUSBAND

Table 4.7 shows how many of the respondents' husbands helped them in their household work. It was found that 24 per

TABLE 4.7: HELP FROM HUSBAND

Response	Block Rait		Block Panchrukhi	
	Respondents	Percentage	Respondents	Percentage
1. Yes	18	24.00	25	33.33
2. No	3	4.00	2	2.67
3. Some times	54	72.00	48	64.00
Total	75	100.00	75	100.00

cent respondents admitted that their husbands helped them in Block Rait and 33.33 per cent respondents in Block Rait and only 2.67 per cent respondents in Block Panchrukhi. In Block Panchrukhi. Further, 4 per cent respondents said that their husbands did not help them at all in. 72 per cent respondents in Block Rait and 64 per cent members in Block Panchrukhi stated that their husbands helped them sometimes. From this analysis, we can say that the majority of respondents' husbands helped them sometimes.

8. PROMOTION OF GIRL CHILD'S EDUCATION

In the present day world, education for girls is as important as boys but this has to be achieved by stressing on this fact among the parents so that they don't feel any difference.

TABLE 4.8: PROMOTION OF GIRL CHILD'S EDUCATION

Response	*Block Rait*		*Block Panchrukhi*	
	Respondents	*Percentage*	*Respondents*	*Percentage*
1. Yes	75	100.00	75	100.00
2. No	-	-	-	-
Total	75	100.00	75	100.00

It was found from Table 4.8 that all 75 respondents promoted girl child's education in Block Rait and the same in Block Panchrukhi. It was heartening to know that in both the Blocks, i.e. Rait and Panchrukhi, the respondents believed in promotion of the education of the girl child.

9. NEWSPAPER READING

One can never undermine the importance of newspaper reading as it makes one aware of happenings in the society. Women Panchayat members must be in the habit of reading

TABLE 4.9: NEWSPAPER READING

Response	*Block Rait*		*Block Panchrukhi*	
	Respondents	*Percentage*	*Respondents*	*Percentage*
1. Hindi	40	53.33	60	80.00
2. English	34	45.34	15	20.00
3. None	1	1.33	-	-
Total	75	100.00	75	100.00

newspaper to keep themselves abreast of what is happening around them. Table 4.9 reveales that 53.33 per cent respondents read Hindi newspaper in Block Rait while 80 per cent respondents in Block Panchrukhi. 45.34 per cent respondents admitted of reading English newspaper in Block Rait and 20 per cent respondents in Block Panchrukhi. Lastly only 1.33 per cent respondents didn't read any newspaper in Block Rait whereas there was none in Block Panchrukhi who didn't read a newspaper. It can be safely said on the basis of the ongoing analysis that majority of the respondents read newspaper whether it be Hindi or English.

10. MEMBERSHIP OF ANY ORGANIZATION

Participation and awareness of women Panchayat members was studied in Table 4.10 to evaluate the respondents. It was found from the Table 4.10 that 2.67 per cent respondents were a member of some professional or occupational association in Block Rait and also the same in Block Panchrukhi. 2.67 per cent women members were found to be members of some community organization—Block Panchrukhi but none in Block Rati. 5.33 per cent members belonged to a religious organization in Block Rait and 6.66 per cent members in Block Panchrukhi.

24 per cent members in Block Rait belonged to some other organization while 54.66 per cent members in Block Panchrukhi belonged to some other organization. 68 per cent

TABLE 4.10: MEMBERSHIP OF ANY ORGANIZATION

Organisation/Association	*Block Rait*		*Block Panchrukhi*	
	Respondents	*Percentage*	*Respondents*	*Percentage*
1. Professional/ Occupational	2	2.67	2	2.67
2. Trade Union	-	-	-	-
3. Labour Welfare Body	-	-	-	-
4. Community Organization	-	-	2	2.67
5. Religions	4	5.33	5	6.66
6. Any other	18	24.00	41	54.66
7. Not associated with any organization	51	68.00	25	33.34
Total	75	100.00	75	100.00

members admitted of not being a member of any organization in Block Rait and 33.34 per cent members stated this in Block Panchrukhi. From the ongoing analysis, it be said that the majority of respondents were not associated with any organization and those who were members of religious or some other organizations.

11. MEMBERSHIP OF A POLITICAL PARTY

Being politically aware is a very important factor for P.R.I. women members. Table 4.11 reveales that 49.33 per cent respondents were members of a political party in Block Rait

TABLE 4.11: MEMBERSHIP OF A POLITICAL PARTIES

Response	*Block Rait*		*Block Panchrukhi*	
	Respondents	*Percentage*	*Respondents*	*Percentage*
1. Yes	37	49.33	44	58.67
2. No	38	50.67	31	41.33
Total	75	100.00	75	100.00

and 58.67 per cent respondents in Block Panchrukhi. 50.67 per cent respondents admitted of not being a member of the Political party in Block Rait and 41.33 per cent respondents in Block Panchrukhi. It was a very interesting analysis that half of the respondents were members of a political party and the other half expressed that they were not a member of any political party in both the blocks—Panchrukhi and Rait.

SUMMARY

To study the empowerment of women rural leadership in Himachal Pradesh as result of the 73rd Amendment Act, the following trends were assimilated and can be summed up as:

1. Women leadership was dominated by Vaishya community.
2. It was found that the majority of women leaders were literate.
3. As far as occupation is concerned, majority of the respondents belonged to the category of agriculturists.
4. The income group of rural women leadership was analyzed to be the lowest income group of below Rs. 50,000.
5. It was heartening to know that women leaders had a small family which had less than five members.
6. The time spent by women leaders in household work was about 6-8 hours daily.
7. The frequency of help from husbands in household to women leaders was found to be low.
8. Encouragingly enough, the majority of women leaders believed in promotion of the education of the girl child.
9. Most of the women respondents read newspaper whether it was Hindi or English.
10. It was interesting to note that most of the women

leaders belonged to some religious organization but not any social or commercial organization.

11. Lastly, 50 per cent of the respondents were a member of a political party.

NOTES AND REFERENCES

1. Bhargava, B.S. (1979), *Panchayati Raj System and Political Parties,* Ashish Publishing House, New. Delhi, p. 12.
2. S.N. Mishra (1977), "Characteristics of Emerging Leadership in Rural India—A Caste Study in a Bihar Panchayat" in *Indian Journal of Public Administration,* Vol. 23, Indian Institute of Public Administration New Delhi, p. 781.
3. C.R. Gada (1977), "Emerging Patterns of Rural Leadership—A Case Study in Gulbarga District" in *Indian Journal of Public Administration*, Indian Institute of Public Administration, Vol. 23, p. 803.
4. S.N. Mishra, *op. cit.,* p. 785.
5. *Ibid.*, p. 787
6. Bhargava B.S. (1979), *op. cit.*, p. 176
7. C.R. Gada (1977), *op. cit.*, p. 803.

5. RELATIONSHIP BETWEEN THE STATE GOVERNMENT AND THE PANCHAYATI RAJ INSTITUTIONS

The revitalization of P.R.Is. has opened new vistas of relationship between the state government and the P.R.Is. For the effective functioning of P.R.Is., sound relationship between the state government and the P.R.Is., has become yet more important and it is expected of both, state government and the P.R.Is. to recognize each other's position and develop a healthy understanding and mutual cooperation to discharge their respective responsibilities.

In the fifty years of democratic governance, a variety of models of development have been experimented to achieve equity, growth and development in the Indian society by the state authorities. Yet the promises of the founder fathers and the goals of our nation have not been realized and the governing machineries have been undergoing stress and strain. The appalling conditions have propelled the leaders of the government to think of an alternative arrangement to manage the existing socio-economic crises and administer development. The fifth decade of Indian Federalism has opened up a new chapter in the annals of institutions of governance in India. Creation of an institutional arrangement at the grass-root level through the Constitution of India for governance with earmarked powers, responsibilities and subject signifies a marked departure from the conventional thinking of federalism. Conventional federalism emphatically establishes relationship between federal and provincial governments. For above four decades the federal polity had undergone a metamorphosis and finally resulted in creating a new institutional arrangement at the bottom of the society for governance. It is almost of a paradigmatic shift from the centre-state relations, which determines the development process of the society. Anyway, the focus has come to the linkages between the state and local bodies.[1]

The introduction of P.R. as a pattern of administration at the district and sub-district levels has raised administrative problems.[2] The administrative challenges to P.R. is not exclusively administrative; it has pronounced politic-psychological overtones. And these make the challenges both intriguing and baffling. It may be argued that the politico-psychological dimension of the challenge is not peculiar to democracy at grass-root level.[3]

Democratic decentralization which has got institutionalized as Panchayati Raj in India is a charter of devolution of power to the people at the rural local levels, who as such, have had no occasion to develop norms of balanced and sober political behaviour through the essentially democratic process of trial, error and correction. This situation, realistically speaking, has potential for these three consequences. First, there is inherent possibility of the non-officials becoming rather sensitive about their sphere of power and authority, they may even develop a tendency to over assert and aggrandize it. Secondly, as politics and power inevitably go together, the phenomenon of politics creeping into the operation of P.R.Is. and its interactive impact on administration can be taken as natural corollaries of a given political situation which may even tend to create in the initial stages, somewhat of an imbalance between the political pre-occupations and developmental obligations of P.R. leadership.

Finally, it also logically follows that there may come about the phenomenon of link politics from bottom upwards with state level politicians and political parties trying to capture and control the power structure from the grass-roots through the district to the state levels and the local politicians making efforts to force patronizing links with higher political echelons.

In a situation of this type, the administration may not merely be exposed to the interaction of local politics. These interactions may become all the more aggressive in a one party dominant system like ours.[4]

For the proper functioning of the Panchayats, mutual cooperation and understanding between the officials and non-official elements is an absolute necessity. Official guidance and advice are as much important to the Panchayats as non-official leadership and initiative.[5]

In any institution, where group effect is involved, the relationship among the members of the group and between the sub-groups is extremely important. This is truer in case of the members working for rural development.[6] Relationship between officials and non-officials is one of the most significant, particularly for the successful day to day working of new institution.[7]

The working of P.R.Is. during the last two years has provided some experiences to assess the official and non-official relationship that has developed during this time. The elected non-officials share, with officials the responsibility for the implementation of development programmes. This is specially so at the Panchayat Samiti and Zila Parishad level where the new local bodies set up at block or taluka and district levels, have been provided with an elaborate official apparatus for implementing the development schemes in various fields.[8]

India's P.R. programme has been analysed from a variety of perspectives both at the time of its inception and at various stages in its evolution. A primary concern of these analyses has been an evolution of roles and relations of officials and non-officials who direct rural development efforts.[9] Writing on the relationship between non-officials and officials, Henry Maddick observes, "One of the most difficult questions in connection with the local government system, is what relationship should exist between officials and non-officials. Ideally, the relationship should be one of popular leadership and the interpretation of the "popular leadership" will be the elected representatives, advising and counselling the officials with whom must rest the execution of the policy, finally adopted. This is a well established pattern in a number of systems but not appreciated in India, better in state government than in the local. It is often said that the politician is responsible for its execution, yet this is an over simplification of the position, for no politician can shut his eyes to the way in which policy is being carried out nor, on the other hand can officers in a developing society avoid offering safe counsel on policy proposals, their alternatives and their consequences.[10]

The ultimate end of Panchayat institutions, being the establishment of self-sufficient and self-governing community, the officials working under them are expected to follow a policy of least interference and maximum encouragement to the management of local affairs by the concerned people. An official is expected to help the non-officials by giving them advice, encouragement, as well as warning. He is expected to play the dual role of taking of initiative himself and evoking initiative in others using his expert skill and experience, in the successful execution of the programme and helping the people to become experts and gain experience, playing the leader and at the same time producing leadership. But when a local institution gains experience and attains maturity, he may slowly withdraw from the scene after entrusting wider responsibilities to the non-officials who are in a better position to assess the local needs and resources and are nearer to the people to evoke their enthusiasm and mobilize their support.[11]

This chapter deals with the relationship between the state government officials and the P.R.Is. The analysis in this chapter is based on the perceptions of the elected representative of the P.R.Is. from the selected sample of the present study.

So far as the relationships between the state government

and the P.R.Is. is concerned, the 73rd Amendment Act does not contain specific provisions in this regard. Article 243 of the Amendment Act provides that subject to the provisions of this Constitution the legislature of a state, may by law endow the Panchayats with such powers and authority as may be necessary to enable them to function as institutions of self-government and such law may contain provision for devolution of powers and responsibilities upon Panchayats at the appropriate level, subject to such conditions as may be specified therein.[12]

Accordingly, the H.P. Panchayati Raj Act, 1994, provides for the functions and powers of the Gram Panchayats (sections 11 to 20), Panchayat Samitis (Sections 81 to 83) and Zila Parishads (Sections 92 to 94).[13] The Act also empowers the state government to add to any of the functions of the P.R.Is. or withdraw the functions and duties entrusted to them [Sections 11(3), 83(2) and 94(2)].[14] This clearly establishes the control of the state government over the functions and powers of the P.R.Is. in Himachal Pradesh.

Under chapter IX of the Act, various provisions of the P.R.Is. in the state have been incorporated. Section 133(1) provides that there shall be a secretary for a Gram Panchayat or a group of Gram Panchayats who shall be appointed by the Director. Section 134(1) provides that in every Panchayat Samiti, the Block Development and Panchayat Officer and in every Zila Parishad the District Development and Panchayat Officer, shall be its secretary.[15] These officers are the appointees of the state government and have the right to attend the meetings of their respective institutions by taking part in the discussions.

The Act under section 137(I) also provides for the state government to authorize any of its officers to inspect all books, proceedings and records and to enter on and impact any work in progress of a Panchayat.[16] Under Article 138(I) of the H.P. P.R. Act 1994 the state government or the prescribed authority may, by an order in writing and for reason to be stated theirin suspend the execution of any resolution passed, order issued, license or permission granted or prohibit the performance of any one by a Panchayat. Section 139(I) of the Act authorizes the state government or the prescribed authority to order in writing, directing the Panchayat to execute any such work in the public interest as is not being executed by it.[17]

Section 140(1) of the Act provides that if at any time it appears to the state government or the prescribed authority that a Panchayat is persistently making default in the performance of the duties imposed on it by or under this Act or under any other law for the time being in force or exceeds or abuses its powers or fails to carry out any order to the state government or the competent authority, the state government or the prescribed authorities may, after such enquiry as it may deem fit, by an order dissolve such Panchayat and may order a fresh constitution thereof.[18]

Section 141 of the H.P. P.R. Act, 1994, also provides that the state government, may, from time to time, cause an inquiry to be made by any of its officers, in regard to any Panchayat matters concerning it or to it any matter with regard to which the sanction approval consent or order of the state government is required by or under this act or the rules made there under or under any law for the time being in force.[19] The prescribed authority under section 145(1) of the Act can suspend any office bearer against whom charges have been framed in any criminal proceedings under various sections of the Indian Penal Code 186 and who has served with a notice along with a chargesheet to show cause under this act, for his removal from the office. Under section 146 of the Act, the state government or the prescribed authority may after such enquiry as it may deem fit to make at any time, remove an office bearer; if he has incurred any disqualification under the act, has been guilty of misconduct in the discharge of his duties adjudged as insolvent, absents from more than half of the meetings convened within a period of six months and if the continuance of such members in office is undesirable in the interest of the public.[20]

All these provisions in the H.P. P.R. Act, 1994 are indicative of the fact that the state government is well equipped to supervise and control the P.R.Is. in the state and these provisions can be serious impediments in the smooth relationship between the state government and the P.R.Is. and also to the autonomy of the new P.R. system which has been termed as a government in itself. In the light of these statutory provisions now the relationship between the state government and the P.R.Is. is being examined on the basis of the perceptions of the elected representatives of the P.R.Is.

Till the '60s Panchayats functioned more as civic bodies. The 73rd Amendment expects the P.R.Is. to become development organizations. Besides civic responsibilities matters listed in the XI schedule can be entrusted to them. The XI schedule contains 29 items beginning with agriculture, land improvement, minor irrigation and ending with public amenities, regulations, regulation of slaughter houses, etc. All the ingredients of an integrated development programme are contained in the XI schedule.[21] In this chapter, an attempt has been made to examine the relationship between the officials and non-officials of the Blocks Panchrukhi and Rait. The relationship was examined on the basis of various parameters which are discussed below.

1. EFFECT OF RELATIONSHIP BETWEEN OFFICIALS AND NON-OFFICIALS ON PERFORMANCE OF P.R.Is.

The Relationship between officials and non-officials has an effect on performance of P.R.Is. So the extent of effect was asked from the respondents. In the Block Panchrukhi, it was revealed from Table 5.1 that 38.67 per cent respondents were highly satisfied with the performance of P.R.Is., 53.33 per cent said that they were satisfied and only 8 per cent expressed that they were dissatisfied with the performance of P.R.Is. whereas in Block Rait, 13.33 per cent were highly satisfied, 80 per cent

TABLE 5.1: EFFECT OF RELATIONSHIP BETWEEN OFFICIALS AND NON-OFFICIALS ON PERFORMANCE OF PRIS

Response	*Block Panchrukhi*		*Block Rait*	
	Respondents	*Percentage*	*Respondents*	*Percentage*
Highly Satisfied	29	38.67	10	13.33
Satisfied	40	53.33	60	80.00
Dissatisfied	6	8.00	5	6.67
Total	75	100.00	75	100.00

were satisfied and only 6.67 per cent were dissatisfied.

The ongoing analysis shows that the majority of respondents were satisfied with the relationship effect on the performance of P.R.Is. and a very few respondents were dissatisfied with it. For establishing sound relationship between the state government and the P.R.Is., it is essential that the officials concerned with the functioning of P.R.Is. cooperate with the latter and render all the administrative assistance, information and advice from time to time. For this purpose, meetings of the P.R.Is. as per the provisions of the Act, are held from time to time. The analysis of Table 5.1 shows that in Blocks Panchrukhi and Rait, the effect of the relationship between the officials and non-officials on performance of P.R.Is. was satisfactory.

2. RELATIONSHIP BETWEEN DISTRICT FUNCTIONARIES AND WOMEN LEADERS OF P.R.Is.

One of the characteristics of P.R. system is that administrative hierarchy runs side by side with different levels of representative institutions. The success of P.R. will depend to a great extent on the proper role of officials and non-officials.[22]

It is revealed from Table 5.2 that in Block Panchrukhi 60 per cent respondents were found to be satisfied whereas only

TABLE 5.2: RELATIONSHIP BETWEEN DISTRICT FUNCTIONARIES AND WOMEN LEADERS OF PRIS

Response	*Block Panchrukhi*		*Block Rait*	
	Respondents	*Percentage*	*Respondents*	*Percentage*
Satisfied	45	60.00	59	78.67
Dissatisfied	10	13.33	11	14.67
Neutral	20	26.67	5	6.66
Total	75	100.00	75	100.00

13.33 per cent were dissatisfied while 26.67 per cent were neutral about it. On the other hand, in Block Rait, 78.67 per cent expressed that they were satisfied with the district functionaries while 14.67 per cent disagreed with it while only 6.66 per cent were neutral. It can be said from the analysis of Table 5.2 that majority of the respondents were happy with the performance of district functionaries.

3. DEVOLUTION OF POWERS TO PRIs AS PER THE NEW H.P. P.R. ACT

Decentralization of powers or devolution of powers takes place in a centralized manner. Decentralization of powers is a major tensional area between the centre and the state.[23] The devolution of powers, authority and responsibility to the P.R.Is. is not only necessary to fulfil the demands, expectations and the aspirations of the people but also to ensure smooth and cordial relationship between the state government and the P.R.Is. In order to assess the position, in this regard, the selected respondents were asked whether the state government was giving powers to the P.R.Is. as per the provisions of the new H.P. P.R. Act.

As per Table 5.3, it indicates that 33.33 per cent were satisfied with the devolution of powers, 40 per cent were dissatisfied whereas 26.67 per cent were neutral in Block Panchrukhi. In Block Rait, a majority of 80 per cent agreed

TABLE 5.3: DEVOLUTION OF POWERS TO PRIS AS PER NEW H.P. P.R. ACT

Response	*Block Panchrukhi*		*Block Rait*	
	Respondents	*Percentage*	*Respondents*	*Percentage*
Satisfied	25	33.33	60	80.00
Dissatisfied	30	40.00	12	16.00
Neutral	20	26.67	3	4.00
Total	75	100.00	75	100.00

that devolution of powers was being done successfully and 16 per cent were dissatisfied while only 4 per cent were neutral.

One of the P.R. activists in his article in the newspaper alleged that so far mass movement in favour of decentralization and local self-government in H.P. has not been able to rise and no serious efforts have been made to create a political atmosphere in the Pradesh in favour of decentralizations. As a result, all the political parties are lacking in political will and are full of contradictions and fear. We have not been able to accept that Panchayats are competent to fulfil their constitutional obligators.[24]

Due to decentralization, the state government and the legislative assembly, are afraid of losing their powers and also fear the emergence of competent Panchayat leadership. Administration and bureaucracy are up in arms against the decentralization and like neither decentralization nor transparency. As such, a major part of the bureaucracy and many trade unions are opposing decentralization. The State Government has failed to coordination between the P.R. Act, rules and the various departmental rules, which are contradictory.[25]

A newspaper report regarding the devolution of powers to P.R.Is. in H.P. states that while the B.J.P. government in H.P. claims to have brought a revolutionary change in the functioning of village Panchayats, these grass-root bodies have been waiting for the past five years for devolution of powers.

The notification of devolution of powers issued in 1996 is being considered as a cruel joke on the Panchayats as none of the departments had so far transferred any of its function to these village level bodies. It was a cosmetic exercise and no responsibility was given to them. [26]

Although all this proves that the process of devolution of powers in H.P. is still on its way, the analysis of the Table 5.3 gives a some what different picture. In Block Panchrukhi, the response was a fractured one with 40 per cent respondents being dissatisfied whereas in Block Rait a majority of 80 per cent respondents were satisfied with the devolution of powers as per the new P.R. Act. One can say that the movement of P.R. has made its inroads on the path of fulfilling the dream of Gandhi of grass-root empowerment.

4. AWARENESS OF DEVELOPMENT PROGRAMMES

Statutory village Panchayats have been constituted not so much in response to local demands as at the initiative of the government. Designed as instruments of rural public administration, Panchayats are expected, among other things to assist the government in carrying out the tasks of rural development. The government has thus both a responsibility and an interest in the development of village Panchayats along the desired lines.[27]

It may be true that the political leaders are committed and

TABLE 5.4: AWARENESS OF DEVELOPMENTAL PROGRAMMES

Response	*Block Panchrukhi*		*Block Rait*	
	Respondents	*Percentage*	*Respondents*	*Percentage*
Yes	22	29.33	35	46.67
No	45	60.00	30	40.00
No Response	8	10.67	10	13.33
Total	75	100.00	75	100.00

identify themselves with broader interests but something more than commitment is needed for them to be effective in their role performance.[28] In tandem with the above discussions, it seems imperative that the political leaders of P.R. must be aware of development programmes so as to fulfil its first and foremost function of rural development. Table 5.4 presents data on this dimension of awareness of development programmes. It was found in Block Panchrukhi that 29.33 per cent respondents agreed that they were aware of the development programmes whereas 60 per cent members of P.R.Is. were not aware of them whereas 10.67 per cent did not respond. On the other hand, in Block Rait 46.67 per cent respondents expressed that they were aware of, while 40 per cent were not and 13.33 per cent respondents did not say anything.

From the above analysis of the Table 5.4, it is indicated that a majority of the respondents were not aware of the development programmes in Block Panchrukhi whereas in Block Rait almost half of the sample population who responded, were aware of the development programmes and half were not. This shows that all political leaders are not aware of these development programmes. So, the government must support and respond to this challenge and hold workshop and seminars to make the rural political leaders aware of various governmental schemes and programmes. Only then, one can expect the rural areas to be developed which is the lifeline of our nation.

5. ROLE OF OFFICIALS IN SPREADING AWARENESS ABOUT DEVELOPMENTAL PROGRAMMES

The day to day concerns of the rural local leadership is with local administration as they are associated with developmental activities. In fact, both the political and administrative wings are equally charged with the responsibility of efficacious administration of community development programmes.[29]

The women local leaders, who have been our respondents, were asked if they were satisfied with the role of officials in spreading awareness about developmental programmes.

TABLE 5.5: ROLE OF OFFICIALS IN SPREADING AWARENESS ABOUT DEVELOPMENTAL PROGRAMMES

Response	*Block Panchrukhi*		*Block Rait*	
	Respondents	*Percentage*	*Respondents*	*Percentage*
Satisfied	43	57.33	19	25.33
Dissatisfied	28	37.33	35	46.67
Neutral	4	5.34	21	28.00
Total	75	100.00	75	100.00

The women P.R.I. leaders in Block Panchrukhi gave their varied opinion regarding this issue. 57.33 per cent expressed their view that they were satisfied with the role of officials in spreading awareness about developmental programmes whereas 37.33 per cent were dissatisfied while only 5.34 per cent were neutral. In Block Rait, 25.33 per cent were satisfied, 46.67 per cent were dissatisfied and 28 per cent were neutral. From the analysis of Table 5.5, it is clear that the responses in Block Panchrukhi were some what different from Block Rait. In Block Panchrukhi out of the sample population, the majority were satisfied whereas in Block Rait only about 25.33 per cent were satisfied. This shows an unbalanced approach of the respondents regarding the role of officials in making the local leaders aware of the development programmes. If the rural leaders are not aware of such programmes how can rural development be expected? The officials should follow a balanced approach in making the local leaders aware so that there is an over all development of all regions and areas at the same time.

6. INTERFERENCE OF STATE GOVERNMENT IN THE WORKING OF P.R.Is.

Close contact, cooperation and coordination between the officials and the non-officials is essential for the successful functioning of the P.R.Is. The ultimate end of the Panchayat institutions being the establishment of the self-sufficient and self-governing community, the officials working under them are expected to follow a policy of least interference and maximum delegation of management of local affairs by the people concerned.[30]

Table 5.6 gives the responses about the interference of state government in the working of P.R.Is. In Block Panchrukhi only 5.34 per cent were satisfied, 21.33 per cent were dissatisfied and 73.33 per cent were neutral about it. On the other hand in Block Rait only 2.67 per cent were satisfied, 17.33 per cent were dissatisfied whereas 80 per cent did not reply at all. The ongoing analysis shows that the majority of respondents did not reply probably because they were not much educated and not aware of the proceedings.[31] It could be that they were getting dominated or influenced by the officials.

TABLE 5.6: INTERFERENCE OF STATE GOVERNMENT IN THE WORKING OF P.R.IS.

Response	*Block Panchrukhi*		*Block Rait*	
	Respondents	*Percentage*	*Respondents*	*Percentage*
Satisfied	4	5.34	2	2.67
Dissatisfied	16	21.33	13	17.33
Neutral	55	73.33	60	80.00
Total	75	100.00	75	100.00

7. AVAILABILITY OF TECHNICAL KNOWLEDGE

The officers must cooperate in the functioning of these institutions and provide necessary technical assistance to the elected representatives so that the latter can function effectively in achieving the maximum good of the people An important initiative was taken in 1979 and that was the inclusion of the industries, services and business (I&B) component in the Integrated Rural Development programme. The main objective of all the programmes of rural development is the alleviation of poverty and elimination of unemployment in the rural areas. For this purpose diversification of rural economy and diversion of rural labour force from the farm sector to the non-farm sector is essential.[32]

Technical skills relevant to the rural areas have to be transmitted on a massive scale to the rural youth and especially the P.R.I. leaders.[33] The development and transfer of appropriate technology is an area where considerable work needs to be done. Once the technology is developed, this is to be disseminated to the field. We asked a sample of 75 women political leaders drawn from Panchrukhi and Rait Blocks in order to know their level of satisfaction about the availability of technical knowledge. As earlier, the format of the question provided three response categories: satisfied, dissatisfied and neutral and each respondent was asked to select the response category that fitted the most with his conception. Table 5.7 presents the leaders' responses to the issue of providing technical knowledge.

TABLE 5.7: AVAILABILITY OF TECHNICAL KNOWLEDGE

Response	*Block Panchrukhi*		*Block Rait*	
	Respondents	*Percentage*	*Respondents*	*Percentage*
Satisfied	37	49.33	11	14.67
Dissatisfied	33	44.00	49	65.33
Neutral	5	6.67	15	20.00
Total	75	100.00	75	100.00

In Block Panchrukhi 49.33 per cent respondents expressed satisfaction. Out of the total sample population, 44 per cent

TABLE 5.8: FREQUENCY OF VISIT BY THE OFFICIALS

Response	*Block Panchrukhi*		*Block Rait*	
	Respondents	*Percentage*	*Respondents*	*Percentage*
Highly Satisfied	31	41.33	10	13.33
Regular	29	38.67	38	50.67
Rarely	15	20.00	27	36.00
Total	75	100.00	75	100.00

expressed dissatisfaction while only 6.67 per cent an insignificant proportion were neutral. In Block Rait, 14.67 per cent out of the total sample population, were satisfied, 65.33 per cent dissatisfied and 20 per cent were neutral about it. It is apparent from the analysis of Table 5.7 that once again both the Blocks presented a different verdict. On one hand, in Block Panchrukhi, almost 50 per cent respondents were satisfied with the availability of technical knowledge whereas in Block Rait much as 65.33 per cent respondents were dissatisfied.

So, monitoring, evaluation, surveillance and a proper feed back system by government and non-government agencies should be made effective so that the women P.R.I. leaders do not feel at a loss to promote development in their area.

8. FREQUENCY OF VISITS BY THE OFFICIALS

For establishing a sound relationship between the state government and the P.R.Is., it is essential that officials concerned with the functioning of P.R.Is. cooperate with the latter and render all the administrative assistance, information and advice to these institutions from time to time. For this purpose, the meetings of the P.R.Is. as per provisions of the Act are held periodically which ought to be attended by the officers of the appropriate level so that necessary information, programs of the various activities undertaken through different departments relating to rural development and the necessary advise is rendered to the elected representatives of the P.R.Is.

The question regarding frequency of visits by the officials to the Panchayats was put up to the respondents. The format of the question provided three categories: highly regular, regular and rarely. In Block Panchrukhi out of the total sample population of 75 respondents, 41.33 per cent expressed that the officials were highly regular in their visits, 38.67 per cent said that their visits were regular and 20 per cent expressed that the officials came rarely.

In Block Rait, only 13.33 per cent said that the officials' visits were lightly regular, 50.67 per cent expressed that the visits of officials were regular whereas 36 per cent said that the officials rarely paid a visit. Once again, both the blocks presented a different picture. Where on one hand, in Block Panchrukhi, a large no. of respondents, as much as 41.33 per cent said that officials' visits were highly regular, on the other hand in Block Rait, 13.33 per cent contradicted it and said that the officials' visits were not at all regular. This discrepancy could be due to lack of cooperation between officials and political leaders in Block Rait. In one of the earlier studies, Gaekwad too refers to similar complaints of indifference of officials in attending the meetings and giving information on the progress of the work to the members of the subject committees. Many officers feel that the officials deliberately behave in this manner just to show their contempt of non-officials.[34]

9. CONTROL OF OFFICIALS OF VARIOUS DEPARTMENTS UNDER PRIs

One of the important aspects determining the relationship between the state government and the P.R.Is. is the command and control of the service institutions, otherwise the service institutions will emerge as the centres of political activity. Nobody rejected totally the view of bringing the staff of the service institutions under the control of P.R.Is. Inspection is the most direct method of exercising governmental control and influence over the Panchayat. A number of officers of the state government have been empowered to inspect the working and examine the records of Panchayats. The officers of the Gram Panchayat Department conduct inspections according to a schedule laid down by the department.[35] So, inspection is the most important method of assessing the work of the Panchayat and in this regard it is the supervisory officers who have to be active to collect information. After the inspection the supervisory staff is expected also to ensure that the Panchayat takes appropriate action to overcome the defects pointed out in the inspection report.

Table 5.9 shows the responses regarding control of officials of various departments under P.R.Is. In Block Panchrukhi, 20 per cent respondents, out of the total sample population, agreed that the control was prevalent and 14.67 per cent respondents said 'no' whereas 65.33 per cent did not reply. On the other hand in Block Rait, 30.67 per cent women P.R.I. leaders said that the control of officials of various departments under P.R.Is. as proper and only 2.66 per cent, a negligible proportion, did not find any control and 66.67 per cent respondent did not say anything.

TABLE 5.9: CONTROL OF OFFICIALS OF VARIOUS DEPARTMENTS UNDER P.R.IS.

Response	*Block Panchrukhi*		*Block Rait*	
	Respondents	*Percentage*	*Respondents*	*Percentage*
Yes	15	20.00	23	30.67
No	11	14.67	2	2.66
Can't Say	49	65.33	50	66.67
Total	75	100.00	75	100.00

From the analysis of Table 5.9 it becomes evident that the majority of the respondents were not sure. Probably they were not much aware of the mechanisms and procedures of government departments and P.R.Is.

SUMMARY

Since the inception of Panchayati Raj official and non-official relationship has been a recurring theme in literature. It is widely felt and not wrongly so, that the success of P.R. depends largely on the balanced relationship between officials and non-officials. The matter of close and friendly relations levels are of great significance in Panchayati Raj since the progress of the massive development programme now being undertaken by these institutions depends largely on such relationships.

The P.R.Is. can emerge as a self-sufficient and self-governing institution only if the officials of the state working with the P.R.Is. follow a policy of least interference and maximum encouragement in the management of the local affairs by the elected representatives of the P.R.Is. However, equally important is the devolution of powers, functions and responsibilities to the local bodies so that they can manage their affairs independently. For a healthy relationship the state government should exercise minimum control over the P.R.Is. The P.R.Is. should get maximum autonomy and powers to deal with the local affairs. In this regard the 73rd Amendment does not provide for any specific check and control over legislature to endow by law such powers and authority to P.R.Is. as may be necessary to enable them to function as institutions of self-government, with such conditions as may be specified therein.

To understand the effect of relationship between the officials and non-officials on the performance of P.R.Is., the respondents were asked whether the women Panchayat leaders were satisfied with their inter-relation and if it affected the working of P.R.Is? It is essential that the relationship must be effective and cordial so that the rural local leaders find it easy to work. It was found that the majority of the respondents were satisfied with that relationships effect on the P.R.Is.

performance.

Secondly, the women rural local leaders of the selected sample were asked about their level of satisfaction with the local functionaries. It was deduced from the analysis of the responses that they were happy with the performance of district functionaries. Thirdly, the issue of devolution of powers to P.R.Is. as per the new H.P. P.R. Act was put up. It came to light that the majority of respondents were satisfied with this issue.

Developmental programmes in the rural areas are very important for advancement and progress in a rural area. The respondents were asked if they were aware of any development programmes and it was found surprisingly that in one block, that is Block Panchrukhi, the women P.R.I. leaders were not aware of the development programmes whereas in Block Rait half of the sample population was aware while the other half was not. This could be because of the government not being active in making people aware of developmental programmes. Further, the respondents were asked if the officials were satisfied with the role of officials in spreading awareness about developmental programmes. Again an unbalanced approach of officials was found as Block Panchrukhi respondents were satisfied whereas only one-fourth of respondent of the sample population were satisfied with the role of officials in spreading awareness in development programme.

Interference of state government in the working of P.R.Is. retards their growth and development. It becomes evident from the analysis of Table 5.6 that in both the blocks, the respondents did not reply to the questions. It could be because they were unaware of this problem or were hesitant in speaking against the state government.

The respondents were then asked if they were made available with the technical knowledge. In both the blocks more than half of the respondents were not satisfied with the role of officials in helping the P.R.I. leaders with technical knowledge. Higher frequency of visits by the officials helps in coordination between the government and the P.R.I. leaders. So the respondents were asked about their satisfaction with their number of visits. Both the Blocks—Panchrukhi, and Rait presented a different picture. In Block, Panchrukhi more than one-third sample population said that they were satisfied with the officials paying them official visits whereas in Block Rait, the respondents were absolutely dissatisfied with the absence of visits of officials.

Finally, the respondents were asked if they were satisfied with the control of various departments under P.R.Is. It was found that the majority of the respondents did not answer, may be because of lack of awareness of the procedures of governmental programmes.

Thus, in a nutshell, one can say about the relationship between the state government and the P.R.Is. that the relationship between the two has strengthened to some extent. Though the state P.R. Act provides enormous powers to P.R.Is. and the latter are also financially dependent upon the state government, the state is also quite slow. Officials concerned with the functioning of P.R.Is. also lack due initiative but still there is a positive reinforcement towards the gap between public authority as manifested in bureaucracy and political leaders as representatives of the common man still persists.

NOTES AND REFERENCES

1. G. Palanithurai (1953), *New Panchayati Raj System at Work: An Evaluation*, Concept Publishing Company, New Delhi, p. 186.
2. Ram K. Vepa (April-June, 1962), "Official Non-Official Relations in Panchayati Raj: The Experience of Andhra Pradesh" in *Indian Journal of Public Administration*, Vol. VII, No. 2, Indian Institute of Public Administration. New Delhi.
3. Iqbal Narain (July-September, 1966), "The Administrative Challenge to Panchayati Raj" in *Indian Journal of Public Administration* Vol. XII, Indian Institute of Public Administration,

New Delhi, p. 564.
4. G. Hargopal (1980), *Administrative Leadership and Rural Development in India*, Light & Life Publishers, New Delhi, p. 155.
5. M.R. Biju, (1998), *Dynamics of New Panchayati Raj System*, Kanishka Publichers, New Delhi 129.
6. G. Hargopal, *op. cit.*, p. 161.
7. Dan Fritz (April-June, 1973), "Evolution of Official and Non-Official Roles in Mysore State and Panchayati Raj" in *Indian Journal of Public Administration*, Vol. 19, Indian Institute of Public Administration, New Delhi, p. 161.
8. Ram K. Vepa, *op. cit.*, p. 186.
9. Dan Fritz, *op. cit.*, p. 161
10. Henry Maddick (1970), "Panchayati Raj—A Study of Rural Local Government in India", Longman, London, p. 260.
11. M.R. Biju, *op. cit.*, p. 130.
12. *Ibid.*, p. 130.
13. The H.P. (1994), Panchayati Raj Act, Directorate of Panchayati Raj, Shimla, pp. 11-14.
14. *Ibid.*, pp. 28-29.
15. *Ibid.*, p. 48.
16 *Ibid.*, p. 49
17 *Ibid.*, p. 50
18. *Ibid.*, p. 50
19. *Ibid.*, p. 51.
20. *Ibid.*, pp. 53-54.
21. V. Padmanabham (1996), "Power to the People—A Shibboleth", in *New Panchayati Raj System: Status and Prospects.*
22. B.S. Bhargava (1979), *Panchayati Raj System and Political Parties*, Ashish Publishing House, New Delhi, p. 325.
23. Palanithurai (1953), *op. cit.*, pp. 99-100.
24. Guman Singh (2000), "This System has not Come up to Expectations", *Amar Ujala*, Chandigarh, p. 4.
25. *Ibid.*
26. *The Tribune* (September 7, 2001), Chandigarh, p. 3.
27. R.C. Prasad (1971), *Democracy and Development*, Rachna Prakashan, New Delhi, p. 220.
28. Shanti Kothari and Ramashray Roy (1981), *Relations between Politicians and Administrators at the District Level*, Indian Institute of Public Administration, pp. 105-106.
29. Iqbal Narain (1976), *op. cit.*, p. 136.
30. M.R. Biju (1998), *op. cit.*, p. 130.
31. For detail See Chapter 6.
32. S.N. Mishra (1989), *New Horizons in Rural Developments*

Administration, Mittal Publications Delhi, p. 48.
33. S.N. Mishra, *Ibid.*, p. 48.
34. V.R. Gaekwad (1969), *Panchayati Raj and Bureaucracy—A Study of Relationship Patterns*, NICD, Hyderabad, p. 44.
35. R.C Prasad (1971), *op. cit.*, p. 226.

6. PARTICIPATORY ROLE OF WOMEN IN DEVELOPMENTAL ACTIVITIES

The representative institution, especially at the grass-root level have been playing a dominant role in the task of development in India, to change the living conditions of rural people by democratic means. In this direction, an initiative was taken by launching the Community Development Programme on October 2, 1952, which provided an opportunity to involve rural people in the development process.

In this chapter, an attempt has been made to evaluate the contributions of elected women representatives in P.R.Is. in performing the duties assigned to them under the 73rd Amendment Act. In order to have a comprehensive viewpoint of the respondents, with regard to participation, these were studied from different angles that are: social, economic, political, educational, public work and civil amenities and trade and commerce. Further, each function was studied on the basis of selected parameters. Information related to these functions have been furnished in Tables 6.1 to 6.6 and discussed as under.

(A) PARTICIPATORY ROLE OF WOMEN LEADERS IN SOCIAL WORK

Panchayats must be recognized as self-governing institutions with domain without interference, control and encroachment.[1] Table 6.1 gives the detail of participatory role of women leaders which included Panches and Gram Pradhans, Up-Pradhans and members of Panchayat Samitis and Zila Parishads. Their role has been studied with the help of different indicators such as, elimination of purdah system, contribution towards the eradication of dowry system, rale in the reduction of violence, participatory role in elimination of the girl child and participation in the c bration of festivals at the community level.

1. Elimination of Purdah System

This system was part and parcel of our society. Women were supported to remain in purdah away from men to avoid any interaction with them. This custom promoted social inequality in the social structure. There is no chance for the welfare of the world unless the condition of the women is reformed. The empowerment of women by itself cannot place women on equal footing with men. The need of the hour is to change social attitudes of women. Information regarding this has been furnished in Table 6.1.

It is evident from Table 6.1 that the majority of elected women leaders' participation in elimination of the purdah system was low. 73.33 per cent respondents and 50.67 per cent members from Block Rait and Block Panchrukhi respectively made a little effort to eradicate this social evil from the society, whereas 20.00 per cent respondents and 30.67 per cent members were of the opinion that they had made some attempt in elimination of the purdah system and remaining only 6.67 per cent respondents from Rait Block and 18.66 per cent respondents from Panchrukhi Block were actively involved in eliminating purdah system from the society.

This analysis shows that a majority of respondents did not involve themselves in eradication of purdah system probably because of their ignorance of ill-effects of this custom.

2. Contribution towards the Eradication of Dowry System

It is ironic that dowry was originally designed to safeguard the women and provision was made in the form of 'Stree dhan'. Stree' means women and 'dhan' means wealth consisting of

TABLE 6.1: PERCEPTIONS OF RESPONDENTS W.R.T. PARTICIPATORY ROLE OF WOMEN LEADERS IN SOCIAL WORK

Indicators	*Block Rait*			*Block Panchrukhi*		
	L	M	H	L	M	H
1. Elimination of Purdah system	55 (73.33)	15 (20.00)	5 (6.67)	38 (50.67)	23 (30.67)	14 (18.66)
2. Contibution towards the eradication of dowry system	28 (37.33)	37 (49.33)	10 (13.67)	5 (6.67)	46 (61.33)	24 (32.00)
3. Involvement in female literacy	11 (14.67)	49 (65.33)	15 (20.00)	7 (9.33)	39 (52)	29 (38.6)
4. Participatory role in the reduction of violence	17 (22.67)	48 (64.00)	10 (13.33)	5 (6.67)	39 (52.00)	29 (41.33)
5. Participatory role in the elimination of female foeticide	22 (29.33)	42 (56.00)	11 (14.67)	27 (36.00)	30 (40.00)	18 (24.00)
6. Particiaption of women leaders of PRIs in the celebration of festivals at community level	25 (33.33)	40 (53.34)	10 (13.33)	9 (12.00)	49 (65.33)	17 (22.67)

money, prosperity or gifts given solely to the women by her parents and relatives at the time of marriage. The abuse of this custom eroded and aborted the original meaningful functions where dowry was a safety not for the women and now it is forcibly made as a price tag for the groom.

An attempt has been made to ascertain the opinion of the elected women representatives about their contribution towards the eradication of the dowry system given in Table 6.1 Out of the total sample population in Block Panchrukhi, 6.67 per cent members expressed that their contribution was low whereas remaining said that their contribution was either medium or high in eradicating this social menace. In Rait

Block, majority of the respondents 49.33 per cent were in the category of medium range while 37.33 per cent said that their contribution was low and remaining 13.67 said that they are highly involved.

This analysis shows that the respondents were somewhat aware and motivated towards eradication of dowry system. The percentage of respondents who were not highly active in this social evil were may be scared of societal pressures and could not muster much courage to revolt against this demonic evil.

3. Involvement in Female Literacy

India has the highest number of illiterates in the world—a mind-boggling estimate of 290 millions of adult illiterates. Literacy is the base of the nations' overall progress and development. We must remember that ignorance leads to greater expectation and lack of empowerment leads to perpetuation of poverty and hunger. India is also known for the best skilled manpower in the world and also for largest number of illiterates in the world. The bane of illiteracy, is prevalent especially among the families with strong political determination and will. Women constitute one-half of our nation's population and because of orthodox and conservative views, females are not given education.

Opinion regarding involvement in female literacy given by the women leaders has been given in the Table 6.1. 65.33 per cent members of the sample population of Block Rait said that they participated in female literacy in their area at a medium level whereas 20.00 per cent members claimed that they actively involved themselves at a high level while 14.67 per cent respondents made a little effort to remove this evil of illiteracy among women. The data of Block Panchrukhi were little varied as only 9.33 per cent respondents involved themselves at a very low level. 52 per cent responded said that they participated at a medium level and 38.6 per cent members made an effort to bring education among females at a high level. The ongoing analysis shows that in both the blocks a majority of them involved in female literacy programmes at medium level and a small percentage participated at a low or high level. One can say that the women P.R.Is. are working in this area but still a lot needs to be done.

4. Participatory Role in the Reduction of Violence

Violence means using force over others to achieve some mala fide intentions. Usually we are faced with violence outside our homes but what about the violence that happens within the four walls of homes. Domestic violence is on the increase but seldom anything is done for this cause.

The members of Gram Panchayats, Panchayat Samiti and Zila Parishad were asked whether they had any role to play in the reduction of violence. The opinion of members is expressed in Table 6.1. It is revealed from the table that majority of the members, that is, 64 per cent respondents participated in the reduction of domestic violence at a medium level whereas 13.33 per cent respondents said that they involved themselves, in this regard, at a high level while as much as 22.67 per cent members did not have much to do with respect to reduction of domestic violence, in Block Rait.

Block Panchrukhi, on the other hand, had a little different response if one analyses from the given Table 6.1. 6.67 per cent respondents expressed that they participated very less whereas 52 per cent respondents stated that they helped people on an average and 41.33 per cent members opined that they involved themselves a lot in the matter of domestic violence reduction. It can be concluded from the above analysis that a majority of women members were active in the reduction of domestic violence.

This analysis shows that most of the women respondents were concerned about the domestic violence in their area and wanted to create a calm and serene atmosphere to develop a peaceful environment for children and family. Progress is not only in economic terms, it also has to be productive in homes to have social progress.

5. Participatory Role in Elimination of the Female Foeticide

In India, we have inherited the cultural legacy of having a preference for sons among all communities, religious groups and citizens of varied socio-economic backgrounds. Patriarchal attitudes manifest in women and girls having subordinate position in the family, discrimination in property rights and low-paid or unpaid jobs. Social discrimination against women results in systematic neglect of women's health, from womb to tomb. The root cause for elimination of female foetus is to be traced in the evil of forced marriages and dowry. Unless illiteracy among the females, is removed the lives of females cannot improve.

In this indicator, the perceptions of the respondents regarding their role in elimination of the girl child has been discussed in the Table 6.1. Out of the total sample population of Block Rait, 29.33 per cent respondents expressed that their participation in this regard was very low whereas 56 per cent members said that they involved themselves at a medium level while 14.67 per cent respondents expressed that their role in this regard was very high. Block Panchrukhi analysis is also not very different. 36 per cent members out of the total sample population opined that they didn't do much about this grave problem whereas 40 per cent respondents expressed that they helped at a medium or an average level while 24 per cent members stated that they participated highly in stopping the elimination of the girl child.

One can say that, from the ongoing analysis, even though one section of the sample population expressed that they didn't do anything actively about it but majority of the women Panchayat members were aware of this serious evil of our society. One can hope that some day this dark phase in the lives of women might be reduced if not over.

6. Participation of Women Leaders of P.R.Is. in the Celebration of Festivals at Community level

Festivals are a part of our Indian culture but in the mad race of today's life, festivals are losing their intrinsic meaning. Commercialization has pervaded into our lives. In villages, people still celebrate festivals at a community level. In Block Rait, out of the sample population, 33.33 per cent respondents stated that they participated in the celebration of festivals at community level very less whereas 53.34 per cent respondents said that they participated to a medium extent and only 13.33 per cent respondents expressed that they took part in the festivals. Block Panchrukhi had a slightly varied response. Only 12 per cent respondents said that they associated with the celebration of festivals at a very low level whereas 65.33 per cent members said that they engaged themselves in the celebration of festivals at a community level and finally 22.67 per cent respondents shared in the celebration. Conclusively, it appears from the data of the above sample that people still celebrated festivals in villages at community level. The women P.R.I. leaders make an effort to do so.

(B) OPINION REGARDING ECONOMIC ACTIVITIES

Economic activities are an integral part of any society. To survive in this world, one needs to develop one's financial potential and acumen to the maximum. In India, now, the times are changing and women are also held to be an important part of the workforce. In rural areas, usually, women are subjugated and suppressed so that men can always have an upper hand. An attempt was made to evaluate the contributions made by women Panchayat leaders in the economic field with regard to their level of participatory role. Table 6.2 gives the detail of the participatory role of women leaders in the economic field.

TABLE 6.2: OPINIONS REGARDING ECONOMIC ACTIVITIES

Indicators	*Block Rait*			*Block Panchrukhi*		
	L	M	H	L	M	H
1. Role in assisting others in seeking employment	18 (24.00)	42 (56.00)	15 (20.00)	31 (41.33)	35 (46.67)	9 (12.00)
2. Knowledge about the preparation of budget	5 (6.67)	37 (49.33)	33 (44.00)	42 (56.00)	27 (36.00)	6 (8.00)
3. Involvement in preparing panchayat budget	20 (26.67)	35 (46.67)	20 (26.66)	35 (46.67)	29 (38.66)	11 (14.67)
4. Checking misappropriation of Panchayat budget	8 (10.67)	36 (48.00)	31 (41.33)	3 (4.00)	32 (42.67)	40 (53.33)
5. Role in discussion of expenditure of school, anganwadis, etc.	7 (9.34)	43 (57.33)	25 (33.33)	12 (16.00)	43 (57.33)	25 (33.33)
6. Role in helping women in getting the right of parental property	38 (50.67)	12 (16.00)	25 (33.33)	27 (36.00)	36 (48.00)	36 (16.00)

1. ROLE IN ASSISTING OTHERS IN SEEKING EMPLOYMENT

Usually in our Indian society, the bread-winner of a family is a man but in the fast changing face of our society, women also have to contribute towards the family income. Educated women in urban areas find it relatively easy to gain employment but in villages, without any awareness for jobs, it is difficult for women to seek work on their own. From Table 6.2 it was found that in Block Rait, women P.R.I. leaders involved themselves in helping women to gain employment,

56 per cent respondents expressed that they participated in assisting others in seeking employment at a medium level whereas 20 per cent respondents stated that their role in the same task was a very significant one.

In Block Panchrukhi, 41.33 per cent women members of the P.R.Is. said that they assisted others to get jobs at a very low level, 46.67 per cent respondents expressed that they helped in this noble cause at a medium level while only 12 per cent respondents expressed the view that they helped others to gain employment at a very high level. From the above data analysis, it can be said that women are becoming aware of economic elevation though at a slow rate.

2. Knowledge about the Preparation of Budget

Women Panchayat members were asked if they had any awareness of how a budget was prepared. This aspect of budget preparation is quite important for Panchayat members to be active in activities of finance. Table 6.2 reveals that in Block Rait 6.67 per cent respondents stated that their knowledge about budget preparation was of a low level whereas 49.33 per cent respondents expressed their opinion that they participated at an average level and 44 per cent women leaders said that they were aware of the budget preparation at a high level. Block Panchrukhi gave quite a different picture. 56 per cent members said that they knew very little about how a budget was prepared while 36 per cent members said that they were aware of budget preparation at a medium level and only 8 per cent respondents admitted of their awareness of budget preparation.

The above analysis of the responses contained in Table 6.2 shows that Block Rait was more advanced in their knowledge of budget preparation. A disparity was found between both the blocks—Panchrukhi and Rait—which must be avoided to remove unbalanced growth.

3. Involvement in Preparing Panchayat Budget

Preparation of Panchayat Budget is one of the major tasks of Panchayat members. The sample population was asked about their involvement in preparing the Panchayat budget. According to Table 6.2, 26.67 per cent members expressed that they didn't involve themselves much in this activity. 46.67 per cent members and 26.66 per cent members said that they participated in budget preparation at a medium and high level respectively in Block Rait. In Block Panchrukhi, 46.67 per cent respondents said that they didn't participate much in budget preparation. 38.66 per cent respondents opined that they involved themselves on an average and 14.67 per cent members responded that they very active in budget preparation.

Analysis of Table 6.2 shows that the women political leaders were not highly active in preparing the budget of the Panchayat.

4. Checking Misappropriation of Panchayat Budget

To check misappropriation of Panchayat Budget, one has to be obviously aware of the procedure of the budget preparation. In Block Rait, 10.67 per cent women members of the P.R. responded that they participated at a very low level in this activity, whereas 48 per cent members expressed that they checked misappropriation of Panchayat budget at a medium level while 41.33 per cent members stated that they checked misappropriation at a high level.

In Block Panchrukhi, only 4 per cent respondents expressed that they didn't check much about budget misappropriation whereas there was a marked difference in the responses in the medium category. 42.67 per cent members responded positively at a medium level and as many 53.33 per cent members said that they checked misappropriation of Panchayat budget at a high level.

The above analysis shows that almost half of the sample population was active in checking misappropriation of budget and the other half was highly active. It shows that they were aware of happenings around them and are against corruption.

5. Role in Discussion of Expenditure of School, Anganwadis, etc.

Schools, anganwadis, etc. are the pillars that strengthen the building of the society. The sample population was asked about their contribution in the discussion of expenditure of school, Anganwadis, etc. According to Table 6.2, in Block Rait, 9.34 per cent respondents said that they didn't involve themselves much in this area, 57.33 per cent members remarked that they discussed about the expenditure of developmental activities at a medium level whereas 33.33 per cent respondents expressed that they were highly involved in such discussion.

Block Panchrukhi had a slightly different picture. 16 per cent respondents said that they didn't bother much about such discussion whereas on the other hand, a very high percentage of 57.33 per cent members said that they played a definite role in the expenditure of schools, etc. 33.33 per cent respondents said that they engaged in discussions of such expenditure.

The above analysis shows that in Block Rait women members of P.R.I. were more alert and conscious about being active in discussions about schools and anganwadis, etc. than Block Panchrukhi. The government must motivate the political leaders to take an interest in such discussions.

6. Role in Helping Women in Getting the Right of Parental Property

In today's scenario, we have been given in our Constitution the fundamental right of equality. With respect to this right, women have an equal right to inherit parental property. An attempt was made to find out if the elected representatives, at the grass-root level, of P.R.Is., participated at all in helping women to get their parental property.

According to Table 6.2, in Block Rait, 50.67 per cent respondents said that they helped in this regard to a very minimal extent, 16 per cent members expressed that they helped other women in this issue to a medium level whereas 33.33 per cent respondents admitted of helping women in getting parental property. In Block Panchrukhi out of the total sample population, 36 per cent members said that they didn't assist women in this area of reference actively, 48 per cent representatives, a very large sample population responded that they participated in this regard to a medium level whereas only 16 per cent respondents expressed that their role in helping women in getting the said right was a high one.

We all know that India has been an orthodox society, throughout the ages and women have never been given an equal status, what to talk about parental property. There has, though, come about a hope of improvement of the situation with women elected representatives. So, it can be said conclusively, on the basis of Table 6.2, that the role of women elected representatives, at all the three levels of P.R.Is., is on the whole on a progressive level. Women seem to be getting more aware of these economic activities as it is the foundation of developmental activities.

(C) VIEWPOINT OF RESPONDENTS VIS-À-VIS POLITICAL PARTIES

Politics is about participation in public sphere but for women's movement both the personal and the public domain are equally political as fluid boundaries separate the public and the private domain.[2] The rich experience of grass-roots organizations of women demonstrates that they do provide a support base to women from marginalized communities as they gain a new identity.[3]

Political consciousness and political equality are two concepts which are gaining a lot of attention these days.

Political parties have an enormous role to play in the social awakening of India. Once Gandhiji told the renowned author Mr. Mulk Raj Anand that we can't build India unless we build villages. Gandhiji wanted to make the villages independent republics, independent in governance and for routine governance, government by the people of villages and self-sufficient for financial needs. Developmental affairs in the rural areas include activities like road building, health centre

TABLE 6.3: VIEWPOINT OF RESPONDENTS VIS A VIS POLITICAL PARTIES

Indicators	*Block Rait*			*Block Panchrukhi*		
	L	M	H	L	M	H
1. Contribution of women representatives in encouraging rural women in developmental activities	24 (32.00)	31 (41.33)	20 (26.67)	25 (33.33)	39 (52.00)	11 (14.67)
2. Involvement in making people aware of their voting rights	6 (8.00)	23 (30.67)	46 (61.33)	15 (20.00)	46 (61.33)	14 (14.67)
3. Involvement in exposing corrupt officials	50 (66.67)	21 (28.00)	4 (5.33)	45 (60.00)	24 (32.00)	6 (8.00)
4. Contribution in making the panchayat system transparent	4 (5.33)	31 (41.33)	40 (53.34)	35 (46.67)	33 (44.00)	7 (9.33)
5. Community participation in awareness of politics	8 (10.33)	27 (36.33)	40 (53.34)	32 (42.50)	35 (46.34)	8 (11.16)
6. Role in encouraging voters to use voter rights with care	4 (5.33)	8 (10.67)	63 (84)	26 (34.66)	35 (46.67)	14 (18.67)

school, opening of cooperatives, etc. Usually, these are left to the government to work on its own. There is very less effort a from the side of women. Table 6.3 indicates about awareness of respondents in political parties.

1. Contribution of Women Representatives in Encouraging Rural Women to Participate in Developmental Activities

Out of the total sample population, in Block Rait, 32 per cent respondents expressed that their contribution in this area was low, 41.33 per cent respondents said that it was medium and 26.67 per cent members stated that it was high. In Block Panchrukhi, 33.33 per cent members expressed that they didn't engage themselves much in this area, 52 per cent respondents stated that they associated at a medium level in developmental activities while only 14.67 per cent respondents said that they involved themselves in such activities at a high level. It may be said that a small percentage of women representatives were involving themselves in developmental activities. It is a long way to reach the goal though a beginning has been made.

2. Involvement in Making People Aware of their Voting Rights

The initial apprehension and doubts over the readiness of womenfolk to come into power-centres and to take up responsibilities of administering development on their own, have been dispelled by their participation in the electoral process of the local body institutions.[4]

Our Constitution makers gave us all voting rights, under the Adult Franchise that we all have the right to vote at the age of 18 years irrespective of caste, colour, creed or religion. In the survey, an attempt was made to evaluate the involvement in making people aware of their voting rights. According to Table 6.3, in Block Rait, 8 per cent respondents expressed that they didn't participate much in this issue of making people aware of their voting rights, 30.67 per cent respondents said that they engaged themselves in this activity at a medium level while 61.33 per cent respondents admitted of helping in this sphere at a very high level. In Block Panchrukhi, 20 per cent women representatives stated that they participated in this activity at a very low level whereas 61.33 per cent respondents said that they associated themselves at a medium level while only 14.67 per cent members expressed that they helped people in this field at a high level.

The given analysis indicates that Block Rait was politically more aware than Block Panchrukhi. A majority of Block Rait women members of P.R.Is. were highly active in making people aware of their voting rights whereas in Block Panchrukhi a very low percentage of respondents were alert about it, may be, because they were themselves not very active politically and were placed there by men, only to gain power.

This disparity between the two blocks of Panchrukhi and Rait could be due to various reasons:

1. *Tradition:* Traditionally, we have a patriarchal family system in which father has been the head of a family and mother's position has been subordinate to him, Further, there is a strong feeling that God had created women for kitchen.
2. *Family Responsibilities:* Family responsibilities have been a handicap for women to actively participate in politics.[5]
3. *Political Parities:* After independence political parties have also failed to educate and mobilize women adequately. They have also aided to provide adequate number of seats for women.[6]

3. Involvement in Exposing Corrupt Officials

Corruption in any form is treated as an incurable disease, a cause of many social and economic evils of society and it damages the morals and ethics of the civilization. Dishonest and corrupt politicians must not be voted to come into power whether he or she belongs to our caste, creed or religion. There must be some penalty and fine on the corrupt officials to have deterrent effects. An attempt was made to find out if the women Panchayat leaders contributed at all in exposing corrupt officials. Out of the sample population, in Block Rait, 66.67 per cent respondents stated that they associated themselves in such activity to a very low level whereas 28 per cent members expressed that they engaged themselves at a medium level while only 5.33 per cent respondents admitted that they involved themselves in exposing corrupt officials.

In Block Panchrukhi, 60 per cent respondents expressed that they didn't involve themselves in this activity whereas 32 per cent members stated that they involved themselves to a medium extent, while only 8 per cent members said that they associated themselves at a very high level. From the above analysis, it can be said that a majority of the sample population did not participate in exposure of corrupt officials may be, from fear. A very low percentage admitted of associating themselves in this activity.

4. Contribution in Making the Panchayat System Transparent

Transparency in administrative system and government is a vital factor these days. In Indian context, the issues between politicians, bureaucrats, criminals and police is a known fact. Corruption has rooted in all walks of life. Every administrative wing is rotten with corrupt practices. The right to know or need of transparency has become too important. Accountability means the responsibility of the administration to the legislature for public expenditure. Accountability, therefore, means not only the submission of accounts of completed expenditure for inspection by the Parliament but also the Parliament's right to criticize public expenditure.[7] So, transparency and accountability are inter-linked as transparency means the citizens' right to know and accountability on the other hand means responsibility of the administration. So, these two concepts lead to reduction of corruption. According to Table 6.3, it became evident that in Block Rait, only 5.33 per cent members said that they played a minimal role in making Panchayat system transparent whereas 41.33 per cent respondents expressed that they engaged themselves in making Panchayat system transparent at a medium level, while 53.34 per cent respondents admitted that they associated themselves in this activity at a high level.

In Block Panchrukhi, 46.67 per cent respondents expressed their role as being less in making Panchayat system transparent whereas 44 per cent respondents said that they involved themselves at a medium level and only 9.33 per cent members stated that they contributed in transparency of Panchayat system at a high level. This analysis shows that Block Rait's elected women representatives contributed in making the panchayat system transparent.

5. Community Participation in Awareness of Politics

Although the Constitution provides for elections before the expiry of 5 years of the first meeting of the elected local bodies, there have been serious delays in many states in the conduct of timely elections. The Supreme Court has laid down the exceptional circumstances in which a slight delay may be condoned as unavoidable but the practice of delaying elections on the other grounds has become regrettably, widespread. This is as true of elections as of bye-elections.

The Constitution stipulates in Articles 243E(4) and 243 U(4), respectively, that if a Panchayat/municipality is dissolved for any reason, elections must be held within six months to reconstitute that particular Panchayat/municipality. This provision is being widely misused to dissolve all Panchayats/municipalities and then avail of the six-month provision to not hold election at all.

States must commit themselves to hold elections within

the stipulated time-period subject only to the exceptional conditions set out in the Supreme Court order.

Complaints of electoral malpractice are widespread. State Election Commission, in consultation with the Central Election Commission, may consider ways and means of riding local bodies' elections of electoral malpractice.[8]

In this context the respondents were asked about their level of awareness at a three merit scale—high, medium, low. The information furnished in Table 6.3 shows that in Block Rait, out of the total sample population only 10.33 per cent respondents admitted that they didn't engage themselves in making people especially women aware in policies, 36.33 per cent respondents said that they associated at a medium level and 53.34 per cent women Panchayat members stated that they involved themselves at a high level. In Block Panchrukhi, 42.50 per cent respondents said that they participated in this activity at a very low level, 46.34 per cent respondents engaged at a medium level and only 11.16 per cent members associated at a high level.

From the ongoing analysis of Table 6.3, it can be said that in Block Rait, half of the sample population participated at a high level and half at a medium level whereas in Block Panchrukhi, a very low percentage participated at a high level and half of the rest participated at a low level and the other half at a medium level.

6. Role in Encouraging Voters to use Voters Rights with Care

Linkages between the State and Local government realms are also produced by the system of party politics. Local democracy does not work in a vacuum but is closely connected to the wider state political framework.[9] Parties have not been a dominant feature of local government and elections have never been organized on party lines. Although elections for the post of the President and the ward members are not contested on party lines, they flaunt their party connections and the members of the same party canvass together as a single group.[10]

So it is very essential that voters are made aware of their rights so that they may use their rights judiciously.

Women Panchayat leaders need to encourage other women to be aware of their voting rights with care. In Block Rait, according to Table 6.3 only 5.33 per cent members admitted that they didn't do much in this regard, 10.67 per cent respondents said that they participated at a medium level and a majority of 84 per cent members stated that they involved themselves at a high level. In Block Panchrukhi, according to Table 6.3, out of the total sample population, 34.66 per cent respondents said that they encouraged other voters to use voter rights with care whereas 46.67 per cent women P.R.I. members admitted that they involved themselves in this activity at a medium level and 18.67 per cent respondents said that they participated at a high level.

From the above analysis, it is clear that in Block Rait, a majority of the respondents involved themselves highly whereas in Block Panchrukhi the percentage was much lower. May be the respondents in this block lacked awareness which the state officials must take care of.

(D) PERCEPTION OF RESPONDENTS VIS-À-VIS EDUCATIONAL ACTIVITIES

Education is a basic amenity and a necessity of our lives. India is wrought with dogmas and superstitions because of lack of education. Now, times are changing and awareness is being brought in the rural and weaker sections of society with the help of women Panchayat members. Education makes a man a source of dissemination of education among the rural masses. An attempt was made to study the perception of respondents regarding educational activities. Table 6.4 furnishes our information vis-a-vis six indicators. They are:

1. Participation in Various Literacy Programmes

Table 6.4 tells us about how much the women Panchayat

TABLE 6.4: PERCEPTIONS OF RESPONDENTS VIS A VIS EDUCATIONAL ACTIVITIES

Indicators	*Block Rait*			*Block Panchrukhi*		
	L	M	H	L	M	H
1. Participation in various literacy programmes	16 (21.33)	35 (46.67)	24 (32.00)	8 (10.67)	42 (56.00)	25 (33.33)
2. Participatory role in providing education to children of weaker sections	17 (22.67)	35 (46.67)	23 (30.66)	21 (28.00)	41 (54.67)	13 (17.33)
3. Participation in preschool and primary school children	25 (33.33)	32 (42.67)	18 (24.00)	32 (42.67)	31 (41.33)	12 (16.00)
4. Involvement in organizing sports and cultural shows	28 (37.33)	32 (42.67)	15 (20.00)	33 (44.00)	32 (42.67)	10 (13.33)
5. Participation in enrolment drive	21 (28.00)	28 (37.33)	26 (34.67)	23 (30.67)	37 (49.33)	15 (20.00)

members contribute towards literacy programmes. Out of the total sample population in Block Rait, 21.33 per cent respondents said that they contributed very less, 46.67 per cent members associated themselves with literacy programmes at a medium level whereas 32 per cent respondents admitted of helping at a high level. In Block Panchrukhi, 10.67 per cent respondents admitted that they didn't contribute much in this field whereas 56 per cent respondents contributed at a medium level and 33.33 per cent respondents engaged themselves in this activity.

This analysis shows that most of the respondents in both the block were active either at medium or high level regarding their participation in various literacy programmes. This means that women leaders take keen interest in social upliftment.

2. Role of Women P.R.I. Leaders in providing Education to Children of Weaker Sections

Children are the future of our society. In urban areas, children get education without much of a problem but in rural areas, it is very difficult to give education to children especially of weaker sections. In Table 6.4 out of the total sample population, in Block Rait, 22.67 per cent respondents admitted that they didn't participate in this area much, 46.67 per cent women Panchayat members stated that they contributed in children's education of the weaker sections at a medium level whereas 30.66 per cent respondents stated that they involved themselves highly in this parameter. In Block Panchrukhi, 28 per cent respondents helped at a low level, 54.67 per cent members admitted of contributing at a medium level, while only 17.33 per cent members engaged themselves at a high level.

The above analysis makes it evident that the majority of women P.R.I. leaders were active in providing education to the children of the weaker sections either at medium or high level. This means that women leaders are a were about their responsible towards the weaker section of the society.

3. Participation in Preschool and Primary School Children

Preparatory schools and primary schools are important stepping stones for children to get further education. It was found from the Table 6.4 that in Block Rait, 33.33 per cent respondents said that they participated in encouraging parents and children for preschool and primary school at very low level whereas 42.67 per cent members involved themselves at medium level while 24 per cent women Panchayat members at a high level. On the other hand, in Block Panchrukhi, 42.67 per cent respondents said that they encouraged parents to send their children to pre-school play ways or also at primary level at a low level, while 41.33 per cent women Panchayat members said that they participated in this activity at medium level whereas only 16 per cent respondents expressed that they participated at high level.

The above analysis shows that majority of respondents in both the blocks—Panchrukhi and Rait—were associated in encouraging pre-school and primary school education at a low or a medium level and only a small percentage were highly active. In fact, it should be the other way round. Goverment has made Primary school education compulsory and free but it has to be ensured that students go to school also. For this, the parents need to be motivated.

4. Involvement in Organizing Sports or Cultural Shows

Sports and cultural shows are a vital part of personality development of children. Table 6.4 furnishes information regarding the contribution of women Panchayat leaders in organizing sports or cultural shows. In Block Rait, 37.33 per cent respondents said that they helped very less, 42.67 per cent respondents admitted of their contribution at a medium level whereas 20 per cent respondents said that they participated in this activity at a high level. In Block Panchrukhi, 44 per cent women Panchayat members responded that they helped very less, 42.67 per cent respondents said that they contributed at an average level while 13.33 per cent respondents engaged at a high level.

This analysis of the data available in Table 6.4 shows that most of the respondents in both the blocks—Panchrukhi and Rait—involved themselves in organizing sports on cultural shows at a low or a medium level. Only a small percentage involved themselves at a high level. This can be interpreted in this way that the majority of the respondents didn't feel that sports and cultural shows were important or were too busy in their own work to spare time for such activities which are an essential part of our lives for all round personality development.

5. Participation in Enrolment Drive of Children in School

According to Table 6.4 in Block Rait, 28 per cent members admitted of contributing in this field at a very low level whereas 37.33 per cent respondents at medium level and 34.67 per cent members at a high level. In Block Panchrukhi, 30.67 per cent respondents said that they helped very less in this area, 49.33 per cent members at a medium level and 20 per cent at a high level.

This analysis of Table 6.4 shows that a very low percentage of the sample population was involved in enrolment drive of children in school. If our younger lot doesn't go to school, we will not have a sound base and a very weak future. A literate and educated India will be a strong economy too in the times to come.

(E) OPINIONS OF RESPONDENTS REGARDING PUBLIC WORK AND CIVIL AMENITIES ACTIVITIES

Activities like construction of roads and drains, installing smokeless chulhas, providing drinking water, construction of community Bhawan, providing sanitation at public places, construction of houses, etc. are very important for development of our rural areas. Table 6.5 gives us data and information regarding the level of contribution made by women Panchayat members.

1. Participation in the Construction of Road and Drainage Facilities

Roads and drains are constructed to develop an area. Table 6.5 furnishes information about the respondents' viewpoint. In Block Rait, 10.67 per cent members said that their involvement in this area was very low whereas 45.33 per cent respondents stated medium level involvement and 44 per cent

TABLE 6.5: OPINIONS OF RESPONDENTS REGARDING PUBLIC WORK AND CIVIL AMENITIES

Indicators	*Block Rait*			*Block Panchrukhi*		
	L	M	H	L	M	H
1. Participation In the system construction of roads and drainage facilities	8 (10.67)	34 (45.33)	33 (44.00)	6 (8.00)	40 (53.33)	29 (38.67)
2. Contibution in installing smokeless chulhas	36 (48.00)	26 (34.67)	13 (17.33)	22 (29.33)	37 (49.33)	16 (21.34)
3. Role in obtaining drinking water for common people	6 (8.00)	43 (57.33)	26 (34.67)	18 (24.00)	43 (57.33)	(18.67)
4. Involvement in construction of Community Bhawan	(9.33)	(58.67)	(32.00)	(12.00)	(44.00)	(44.00)
5. Contributionin providing sanitation at public places	(13.33)	(49.33)	(37.34)	(14.67)	(64.00)	(21.33)
6. Involvement in construction of houses	(50.67)	(17.33)	(32.00)	(16.00)	(52.00)	(32.00)

respondents expressed a high level participation. In Block Panchrukhi, only 8 per cent respondents admitted of not doing much in this field whereas a majority of 53.33 per cent respondents stated a medium level participation while 38.67 per cent respondents admitted of high level contribution.

This ongoing data analysis shows that a majority of respondents were involved in construction of roads and drainage in both blocks which is a very encouraging picture as roads as well as drainage form an integral part of development at the grass-root level which was the basic purpose of P.R.I. formation.

2. Contribution in Installing Smokeless Chulhas

According to Table 6.5, in Block Rait, 48 per cent respondents' contribution was very low with respect to installation of smokeless chulhas whereas 34.67 per cent respondents, was medium while 17.33 per cent respondents was high. In Block Panchrukhi, 29.33 per cent members contributed at low level, 49.33 per cent respondents at medium level and only 21.34 per cent members at high level.

The ongoing analysis of the data given in Table 6.5 shows that the elected women representatives of P.R.Is. involved themselves in the installation of smokeless chulhas at either low level or at a medium level.

In fact, smokeless chulhas are very useful as they avoid pollution and are environment-friendly but sadly, our respondents did not participate in this activity highly.

3. Role in Obtaining Drinking Water for Common People

Clean drinking water is lifeline for healthy life. Table 6.5 gives us a picture about the levels at which the elected women representatives contributed in obtaining drinking water for common people. In Block Rait, out of the total sample population, only 8 per cent respondents said that they helped at very low level whereas 57.33 per cent respondents expressed that they participated at medium level, while 34.67 per cent respondents associated themselves at high level. In Block Panchrukhi, 24 per cent respondents stated that they involved themselves at low level whereas 57.33 per cent respondents admitted of engaging themselves in this activity at medium level, while 18.67 per cent respondents at high level.

This data analysis given in Table 6.5 once again shows that our women elected representatives do not have an important role in obtaining and providing drinking water for common people. Majority of the respondents of the sample population fell in the medium level category whereas it should have been at high level as clean drinking water is very important for a healthy population. Dirty drinking water leads to diseases and unhealthy life. This kind of environment further is conducive to unproductive manpower. So, to achieve an optimum utilization of manpower, women political leaders must be pro-active in this area.

4. Involvement in Construction of Community Bhawan

In villages, a Community Bhawan helps in hosting various religious and social functions. Table 6.5 shows that the respondents involved themselves in this activity at various levels. In Block Rait, out of the total sample population, only 9.33 per cent respondents admitted of not doing much in this activity. A majority of 58.67 per cent respondents admitted involvement at medium level while 32 per cent members expressed at high level. In Block Panchrukhi, only 12 per cent respondents stated that they participated in this activity at low level, 44 per cent respondents at medium level whereas 44 per cent respondents at high level.

The above data analysis of Table 6.5 shows that a majority of respondents were quite active at high level in the construction of Community Bhawan. This means that even though the sample population was not very active in areas like education, provision of drinking water and smokeless chulhas, etc., they liked religious and social activities, due to this they take keen interest in the construction of Community Bhawan.

5. Contribution in Providing Sanitation at Public Places

According to Table 6.5, 13.33 per cent respondents said that they involved themselves in providing sanitation at public places at very low level whereas 49.33 per cent respondents said that they participated at medium level, while 37.34 per cent members said that they associated themselves with the activity at high level. In Block Panchrukhi, out of the total sample population 14.67 per cent members admitted of not involving themselves much in this activity, 64 per cent respondents stated of medium level participation, while 21.33 per cent respondents involved themselves at high level.

This analysis of Table 6.5 shows that the majority of the respondents fell in the medium level which means that they are quite conscious and aware of the problem of sanitation at public places and want a clean and healthy environment to promote health as opposed to their lack of concern with the provision of clean drinking water. This could be due to their lack of knowledge and awareness about the usefulness of clean drinking water which the administrators must provide.

On the other hand, the majority of the sample population was pro-active in the provision of sanitation at public places.

6. Involvement in Construction of Houses

Table 6.5 shows to what level the women elected representatives of P.R.Is. contribute in construction of houses for downtrodden people. In Block Rait, 50.67 per cent respondents confessed of low participation whereas 17.33 per cent members admitted of medium level participation, while 32 per cent members expressed that their involvement was of high level. In Block Panchrukhi, 16 per cent members admitted of low participation, 52 per cent members said that they engaged themselves at medium level while 32 per cent members stated that they associated themselves at high level.

The above analysis of Table 6.5 shows that both the blocks—Panchrukhi and Rait—had a different response. In Block Panchrukhi, women political leaders were associated with construction of houses for the poor at medium level whereas a majority of Block Rait respondents confessed of low participation. The officials must motivate Block Rait political leaders to come forward and develop their area by making them aware of various development housing schemes.

(F) PERCEPTION OF RESPONDENTS AS REGARDS TO TRADE AND COMMERCE

Trade and commerce is one of the most important economic activities for any area's development. In Table 6.6 it was attempted to gauge how and to what level the women Panchayat members contributed to raise the level of trade and commerce of their area.

The success of development programmes also depends on the will of the political and administrative elite to decentralize real power at the grass-root level. The choice in the matter is thus very sharp in view of the disintegration of the fabric of the Indian society. Either decentralize or perish. Without decentralization there is neither going to be democracy nor economic development. If both are denied, it is obvious that the logic of the rest of the system will push it towards authoritarianism on the one hand and acute exploitation and inadequacies on the other.[11]

1. Role in Organization of Cooperative Marketing of Agricultural and Other Products

Rural areas have the capability to produce crops and even manufacture products though at a small scale but don't have the acumen of marketing it. Table 6.6 shows the involvement of the respondents In Block Rait, out of the total sample population, 33.34 per cent respondents stated that they helped in this area at a low level, 60 per cent members responded medium level and only 6.66 per cent members admitted of high level participation. In Block Panchrukhi, 68 per cent respondents admitted of low participation. 22.63 per cent respondents expressed medium participation and only 9.33 per cent members said that they contributed high level participation.

From the ongoing analysis of Table 6.6, it becomes quite evident that the majority of the respondents of the sample population belonged either to low or medium category. This

TABLE 6.6: PERCEPTION OF RESPONDENTS AS REGARDS TO TRADE AND COMMERCE

Indicators	***Block Rait***			***Block Panchrukhi***		
	L	*M*	*H*	*L*	*M*	*H*
1. Role in organization of cooperative marketing of agricultural and other products	25 (33.34)	45 (60.00)	51 (6.66)	51 (68.00)	17 (22.63)	7 (9.33)
2. Association with providing cheap credit facilities to people	35 (46.67)	35 (46.67)	5 (06.66)	29 (38.67)	40 (53.33)	6 (8.00)
3. Contribution in Checking malpractices	45 (60.00)	23 (30.67)	7 (9.33)	26 (34.67)	34 (45.33)	15 (20.00)
4. Role in maintenance of cooperative godowns	51 (68.80)	14 (18.67)	10 (13.33)	50 (66.67)	17 (22.67)	8 (10.66)
5. Contribution in organization of cooperative consumer societies	50 (66.67)	20 (26.66)	5 (6.66)	52 (69.33)	10 (13.33)	13 (17.34)
6. Participation in procurement of remunerative prices	51 (68.00)	19 (25.34)	5 (6.66)	48 (64.00)	18 (24)	9 (12)

means that the women leaders were not very active in providing the facility of Cooperative Marketing of Agricultural and other products to the farmers.

The officials must see to it that the farmers get the knowledge of cooperative marketing which is quite beneficial to all concerned as it will help them to send their products and crops to the markets at reasonably good prices.

2. Association with Providing Cheap Credit Facilities to People

Role of Credit Agencies—Development of rural sector involves integrated efforts of credit and non-credit institutions. Credit institutions have been increasing their involvement in the developmental process, year after year. In order to highlight the role of various credit agencies and to ensure a proper direction to the credit, Reserve Bank of India had introduced the system of Lead Bank Scheme, which devolves the responsibility of planning and monitoring of credit to the Lead Bank of the district.[12]

Thus, P.R.Is. could effectively augment their resources through appropriate utilization of bank finance for poverty alleviation programmes as well as area/infrastructure development.

In today's world of plastic money, credit facility is a way of life in urban areas but it has not permeated down to the rural areas. In this survey, an attempt has been made to see to what level cheap credit facilities to people are being given to rural people by elected women Panchayat members. According to Table 6.6, in Block Rait, out of the total sample population, 46.67 per cent respondents confessed of low participation whereas 46.67 per cent respondents admitted of medium level contribution while only 6.66 per cent members said that they engaged in this activity at high level.

In Block Panchrukhi, 38.67 per cent members helped at low level, 53.33 per cent respondents contributed at medium level and only 8 per cent respondents admitted of high level contribution. From the ongoing analysis it can be concluded that a very low level of women members of P.R.Is. contributed in the field of providing credit facilities to people in rural areas.

3. Contribution in Checking Malpractices in Trade and Commerce Activities

It was found from Table 6.6 in Block Rait that 60 per cent members contributed at low level, 30.67 per cent respondents involved themselves at medium level and only 9.33 per cent members engaged at high level. In Block Panchrukhi, 34.67 per cent members involved themselves at low level whereas 45.33 per cent respondents associated themselves in this activity at medium level while only 20 per cent members helped in checking malpractices at high level. According to this analysis, it appears that a very low percentage of respondents contributes in checking malpractices in trade and commerce. This could be due to lack of knowledge and awareness about trade and commerce activities. The government should keep a supervisory control over the officials so that they provide such knowledge to the women political leaders.

4. Role in Maintenance of Cooperative Godowns

Cooperative societies are a landmark in the development of our rural society. Godowns are its practical aspect which helps in their functioning. Table 6.6 furnishes the data of the level of the role of women P.R.I. members in the maintenance of godowns. In Block Rait, out of the total sample population, 68.80 per cent members admitted of low role, 18.67 per cent members confessed of a medium role whereas only 13.33 per cent members said that they contributed at high level. In Block Panchrukhi, 66.67 per cent members stated that they contributed at low level, 22.67 per cent members admitted of medium level contribution and only 10.66 per cent members confessed of a high level contribution in this field.

According to the ongoing analysis, it becomes clear that

the majority of the sample population did not have a key role in maintenance of cooperative godowns. This could be because of unawareness and lack of interest in such activities or these were no godowns. To speed up the movement of P.R.Is., officials and functionaries must promote the concept of cooperative godowns so that they can have benefit of storage of their crops or products. This way, the crop can be kept safe from adverse weather conditions and from any thefts also.

5. Contribution in Organization of Cooperative Consumer Societies

In planned development, cooperation is an instrument which, while retaining some of the advantage of decentralization and local initiative, will serve willingly the purpose of the five year plans. The main objectives of the cooperative societies is to raise funds by deposit from members and loans from government and distribute the money thus obtained as loans to members.[13] According to Table 6.6 It was found from the respondents that in Block Rait, 66.67 per cent members said that their contribution in this respect was of a low level whereas 26.66 per cent members confessed of a medium level participation and only 6.66 per cent respondents stated that they helped in this area.

Block Panchrukhi didn't give a very different picture. 69.33 per cent members admitted that they contributed at low level, 13.33 per cent respondents expressed medium level participation while only 17.34 per cent respondents said that they helped at high level.

This ongoing analysis of data shows that most of the respondents of the sample population were contributing either at low or medium level. The women P.R.I. leaders were not active in cooperative consumer societies organization. This could be due to lack of knowledge about consumer cooperative societies, in which the role of officials concerned also is to be criticized.

6. Participation in Procurement of Remunerative Prices

To get a reasonable price for the produce of rural people, women Panchayat members need to help in this field so that the role of the middle-man is eliminated. According to Table 6.6, in Block Rait, as many as 68 per cent members admitted of low participation whereas 25.34 per cent members confessed of medium participation while only 6.66 per cent respondents said that they involved themselves of a high level participation. In Block Panchrukhi, 64 per cent respondents answered that their role in this activity was low whereas 24 per cent members admitted of a medium level participation while only 12 per cent respondents confessed of high level participation.

The above analysis shows that very low percentage of women Panchayat members associated themselves at high level in procurement of remunerative prices. Majority of the respondents confessed of low level participation. As a whole, this means that the respondents' participation in trade and commerce was low. This area needs special attention so that these two blocks can become economically strong.

SUMMARY

Participatory role of women leaders of P.R.Is. was studied on the basis of the data collected from the respondents. The survey was conducted on six basic parameters to understand the contribution of the women leaders. They were:

1. Social Work

It entailed elimination of purdah system, eradication of dowry system, female literacy, reduction of domestic violence, eradication of elimination of the girl child and celebration of festivals at a community level. From the analysis of Table 6.1, it can be concluded that a majority of women leaders contributed in limitation of purdah system only at minimal level and only a few were highly aware of their social responsibilities. Again it was found that only a small percentage actively contributed in the eradication of dowry system whereas a majority of them helped in female literacy programmes at a medium level while a lesser percentage were activity involved.

As far as their role in reduction of violence is concerned, most of them contributed again at medium level while a small percentage were highly involved in the avoidance of elimination of the girl child whereas the majority of them involved themselves at medium level. Finally, one can say that the participation of a majority of women members in the social work was of a medium level.

2. Economic Activities

The foregoing analysis reveals that on an aggregate level, the majority of the respondents expressed medium level participation in economic activities. This parameter was evaluated at six diversified fields:

Firstly, the role of elected women representatives at P.R.I. level was assessed in assisting others in seeking employment and it was found that the majority of the respondents helped at medium level while a small percentage helped at high level.

Secondly, their knowledge about the preparation of budget was evaluated which was a little different from the earlier indicator. Both the Blocks, Rait and Panchrukhi, gave a different analysis. In Block Rait, a high percentage of respondents were highly aware of budget preparation whereas a small percentage were aware only at low level.

Thirdly, their involvement in the preparation of budget was studied which gave the result that a majority participated at medium level. The fourth indicator was their contribution regarding checking misappropriation of Panchayat budget. Majority of the respondents admitted of a high level contribution. The fifth indicator involved in the discussion of expenditure of school, anganwadis, etc. in which a majority of respondents said that they discussed budget of Panchayats at medium level.

The sixth indicator was the role of women Panchayat members in getting the right of parental property. The block-wise analysis was quite different. In Block Rait the maximum respondents were not very active in this regard whereas in Block Panchrukhi the majority helped at an average level. So, it can be safely said that the respondents were involved in economic activities at medium level.

3. Political Activities

From the analysis of Table 6.3, it can be observed that a majority of respondents were quite active in making people aware of their political rights. Political awareness is an essential element of democracy. Firstly, it was found that women Panchayat members' contribution in encouraging rural women to participate in developmental activities was mostly at medium level and a low percentage were involved highly. Secondly, again a majority were involved in making people aware of their voting rights at medium level in Block Panchrukhi whereas in Block Rait, the majority participated at high level. Thirdly, a majority responded said that they associated themselves in exposing corrupt official at low level.

Fourthly, a majority of the respondents didn't contribute much in making the Panchayat system transparent. Fifthly, community participation in awareness of politics was difficult as Block Rait showed a high level of participation whereas Block Panchrukhi was absolutely opposite with a low level participation. Sixthly, if one sees block-wise, the response was quite varied with reference to encouraging voters to use voter's rights with care. In Block Rait, the respondents said that they participated highly whereas in Block Panchrukhi, it was found, to the contrary, that a low percentage of respendents contributed highly in this activity.

4. Educational Activities

The contribution of women Panchayat members was assessed

from Table 6.4 in educational activities. Firstly, as far as participation in various literacy programmes is concerned a majority of respondents participated at medium level and a major portion of them were highly active. Secondly, their role regarding education to children of weaker sections was again gauged at an average level. While the third indicator of their participation in providing education to preschool and primary school children showed that the respondents helped at medium level and a lower percentage at a higher level. Fourthly, the involvement of respondents in organizing sports or cultural shows was found to be again of a medium range. The fifth, the last indicator, dealt with the enrolment drive of children in school. The respondents conformed to the trend of medium level response.

5. Public Work and Civil Amenities Activities

Firstly, the participation of women Panchayat members regarding construction of road and drainage facilities was found to be of high level in both the blocks. Secondly, their contribution in installing smokeless chulhas was gauged at low level. Thirdly, their role in obtaining drinking water for common people was analyzed as medium whereas fourthly their involvement in construction of a Community Bhawan was also found to be of an average level. The Fifth indicator, concerning provision of sanitation of public places, according to the analysis, showed that a majority of respondents contributed at a medium level. Lastly, the Sixth indicator dealt with the involvement in construction of houses for down trodden in which most respondents expressed a medium level range and a lower percentage participated at high level in Block Panchrukhi whereas a majority of respondents in Block Rait said that they helped at low level.

6. Trade and Commerce

After going through the statistical analysis of Table 6.6, it came to light that in both the blocks and all the six indicators involving:

- Organization of cooperative marketing of agricultural and other products.
- Providing cheap credit facilities to people.
- Checking malpractices
- Maintenance of cooperative godowns
- Organization of cooperative consumer societies and
- Procurement of remunerative prices.

The majority of respondents showed that they contributed at low level and a very small percentage participated at medium or high level.

NOTES AND REFERENCES

1. D. Bandyopadhyay and Amitava Mukherjee (2004), *New Issues in Panchayat Raj*, Concept Publishing Company, New Delhi, p. 96.
2. *Ibid.*, pp. 64-65.
3. *Ibid.*, p. 65.
4. G. Palanithurai (1999), *op. cit.*, p. 55.
5. C.P. Bhartwal and Kumkum Kishore (2003), *Public Administration in India*, A.P.H. Publishing Corporation, New Delhi, p. 328.
6. *Ibid.*, p. 329.
7. D. Bandyopadhyay and Amitava Mukherjee, *op. cit.*, p. 34.
8. Sanjeev K. Mahajan (Jan.-Dec., 04), *Public Accountability of State Level Public Undertakings in India: A Case Study in Dynamics of Public Administration*, Department of Public Administration, University of Lucknow, p. 22.
9. C.P. Bhartwal and Kumkum Kishore, *op. cit.*, p. 270.
10. *Ibid.*, p. 270.
11. S.L. Goel and Shalini Rajneesh (2003), *Panchayati Raj in India : Theory and Practice*, Deep & Deep Publications Pvt. Ltd., New Delhi p. 184.
12. *Ibid.*, p. 200.
13. S.K. Mahajan (1984), "Some Aspects of Personnel Management in the Kangra Central Cooperative Bank Limited with special reference to Dharamshala Head Office", Unpublished Dissertation submitted to Department of Public Administration, Panjab University, Chandigarh.

7. CONCLUSION AND SUGGESTIONS

The concept of local government or Panchayat has filtered down from the Vedic times and this we know from the historical accounts. Villages and their administrative system have continued till today with minor variations intact in their concept. At the grass-root level, village was an economic as well as an administrative unit.

Presently, local government in India consists of two broad categories—Rural and Urban as a result of Constitutional Amendments in 1992. The full benefit of development can only be realized with full participation and the role of women can not be isolated from the total framework of development as they constitute half of the population. A review of the economic roles played by women in India shows that the traditional village community of India consisted of the cultivators, the artisans and those performing menial services in which women played a distinctive and accepted role in the process of earning a livelihood for the family in both the marketing of products of agriculture and handicrafts.

Since, the Decade of Women (1975-85) women's development has been conceptualized by equity, empowerment and rights-based approaches, with varying emphasis on concerns like the condition/situation and the practical or strategic needs of women. A major drawback in this welfare approach was that women were net recipients and not participants in the agencies and programmes created for their own development. Then came the 'Empowerment Approach' through which gender bias could be eliminated and women could be a part of their own development schemes and projects.

In the Constituent Assembly of 1950, as well as in the

Equality Report in 1974, women leaders rejected the notion of 'Quota' in the political decision-making process. The National Perspective Plan (1988-2000), after a decade or so, categorically recommended 30 per cent of seats to be reserved for women in Panchayats. Finally, the 73rd and 74th Amendment Acts (1992) had a provision of reserving not less than 33% per cent the total seats for women, both at the functionary as well as membership level. It is imperative to note here that within a span of 10 years, about 5-6 million women have come to active politics by the cause of reservation of seats in local government institution.

In the pervious chapters an attempt has been made to analyse in detail of the outcome of empowerment of women in Panchayati Raj institutions in Himachal Pradesh as a consequence of the 73rd Amendment of the Constitution. The present chapter focuses the major findings of the study with some suggestions to improve the existing arrangement.

The present study is based on the basic assumption or hypothesis that the women leaders have failed to perform their duties at the grass-root level. The hypothesis was further divided into sub-hypotheses:

(i) Low literacy and lack of knowledge amongst women leaders have resulted in non-performance of their role.

(ii) The negligence and indifferent attitude of executives towards women leaders have resulted in dissatisfaction amongst them.

Findings of the present study reveal that despite deep-rooted systemic, cultural and political resistance, women have demonstrated the potential of challenging the problems of the society. The elected women representatives are engendering the development process at the grass-root level with enabling support and capacity building by civil society agencies and women's groups. The representation of six million women in the P.R.Is., directly and indirectly, has given inputs to the processes of social mobilization. The new leadership of the P.R.Is. has substituted the old rural leadership.

FINDINGS OF THE STUDY

The Panchayati Raj is an ancient concept which has a long history in India. These are the oldest administrative institutions in our country. During Vedic era, powers vested in the hands of people and the organization was known as 'Panchayati System'. Description of Panchayats is available in famous books, such as *jatakas*, *Ramayana* and Kautilya's *Arthashastra*. As time passed by, they were brought under control of the king after which the village assembly lost much of its power and prestige but still certain matters were discussed in this assembly. Also, it was the connecting link between the village and central administration. The institution of local self-governments received considerable attention during the British rule but the focus was entirely on the urban bodies. Mahatma Gandhi's vision of Gram Swaraj led to a consensus and a provision was made in the Constitution under the Directive Principles of State Policy in Article 4 which emphasized on the powers and authority to be vested in village Panchayats. It was found in the study that in 1948, Jawaharlal Nehru while inaugurating the conference of the ministers on Local Self-Governments in the provinces, said, local self-governments is and must be on the basis of any true system of democracy. Democracy must be built from below and not at the top. In 1882, the Government of India Resolution, for the first time, directed local governments to set up rural boards similar to municipal boards. Then in 1907, in the Report of the decentralization, it was said that an inquiry must be made into the financial and administrative relations of the government of India and the provincial governments that, it was found later in 1952 and 1953, two programme Community Development and National Extension Services, were launched respectively, but they failed to achieve their development objectives. Then came the Balwantrai Mehta Committee Report in 1957. The creation of P.R. in 1959 was held as a revolution. The Committee emphasized that there should be a three-tier structure of local self-governing bodies from the village to the district, adequate powers may be entrusted to these bodies to avoid excessive state control, all developments programmes to be executed through these bodies, etc.

So, these P.R.Is. became mainly executive agencies for the national and state plans. Then came the Ashok Mehta Committee Report in August 1978 and made 132 recommendations. The main recommendations that can be noted are that there should be a two tier set-up in the P.R. structure, i.e. a district level, Zila Parishad and a Mandal Panchayat covering a population of 15,000 to 20,000, the term of P.R.Is. to be four years and direct elections to be held simultaneously, a permanent grant of amount not less than Rs. 2.50 per capita should be made to the Mandal Panchayats, etc. Ashok Mehta Report has made an attempt to revitalize the P.R. system as established according to the reconsiderations of Balwantrai Mehta Report.

It was highlighted during the study that there were a few more landmarks like the Chief Minister's Conference in 1979, Dantwala Committee in 1977, the phase of revival (1983) onwards, L.M. Singhvi Committee in 1986 and Sarkaria Commission in 1988. Then finally came the 73rd Constitutional Amendment Act in 1992 with effect from 24th April, 1993 which conferred constitutional status to Panchayats and government from the village upwards.

It was also found that the P.R. system in the H.P. was established in a statutory form under the provisions of the H.P. P.R. Act, 1952 in the year 1954. The number rose from 280 Gram Panchayats before the enactment of the H.P. P.R. Act, 1952 to 2922 Gram Panchayats. 71 Panchayat Samitis and 12 Zila Parishads as on 10-03-1999. In the chapter of Organizational Structure of Panchayati Raj Institutions in Himachal Pradesh, it was found that sound organizational structure is an essential key for the success of an organization to a systematic bringing together of inter-dependent parts to form a unified whole through which authority, coordination and control may be exercised to achieve a given purpose.

It was found in detail about the various important sections given in the H.P. P.R. Act, 1994. Section 3 declared that the government could declare by notification any village or group of contiguous villages with a population of not less than one thousand and not more than five thousand to constitute one or more sabha areas. The government could also increase, diminish or alter any sabha area. Section 4 dealt with the establishment of Gram Sabha by name in every area in which there would be a list of voters whose names would be entered but in not more than one Gram Sabha area. Every Sabha was to hold four general meetings in each year. The quorum of such general meetings would be representation of at least one-third of the total number of families represented by one or more members of the Gram Sabha.

Section 7 dealt with the functions of Gram Sabha, which entitled mobilizing voluntary labour and contribution in kind and cash for the community welfare programmes, identification of beneficiaries for the implementation of development schemes pertaining to the village promotion of unity and harmony etc.

Section 7-A dealt with the Constitution of Up-Gram Sabha for each ward of a Gram Sabha with its details also regarding its general meetings, venue and time of the meetings, nomination of its members, etc. Further Section 8 as associated with the Constitution of Gram Panchayats and seat reservation and Section 9 with the meetings of the Gram Panchayats. Section 10 dealt with the maintenance of Gram Panchayat records and Section 11 with its functions. Section 12 and 13 was connected with the power of removal and nuisance and to make general orders.

Section 77 stated about the establishment of Panchayat Samiti and its Constitution. Sections 79, 80 and 81 dealt with the election of Chairman and Vice-Chairman of the Panchayat Samiti and its functions. Sections 82 to 87 dealt with standing committees and its procedures and establishment of Zila Parishad. Section 93 dealt with the functions of the State Government to a Zila Parishad and Section 94 with the power of the State Government in relation to functions of Zila Parishad.

The next chapter dealt with the socio-economic background of elected women representatives of P.R.Is. It was found that women leadership was dominated by Vaishya Community and was literate. As far as occupation was concerned, majority of the women elected representatives belonged to the category of agriculturists and the income group of rural women leadership was analysed to be the lowest income group of below Rs. 50,000. Most of the respondents had a small family which had less than five members and the time spent by them in household work was about 6-8 hours daily. Their husbands helped in household work only some times. It was very encouraging to note from the analysis of the data that the majority of women leaders believed in promotion of the education of the girl child. The women leaders were quite aware as far as newspaper reading was concerned. Each one of them read a newspaper whether in Hindi or English. They belonged to some religious organization and half of the sample population was a member of a political party.

In the chapter of 'Relationship between the State Government and the Panchayati Raj Institutions', it was observed that the rural local leaders found their performance satisfactory and it was easy to work as a consequence of good relationship between the officials and non-officials. Further, it became evident that the rural local leaders were happy with the performance of local functionaries. Again, the respondents were satisfied with the devolution of powers to P.R.Is. as per the new Himachal Pradesh Panchayati Raj Act. Otherwise, it is usually found that decentralization of powers is a major tensional area between the state and the centre. Here, it was found, encouragingly, that the political leaders were happy.

It was found, during the study, of the most common and controversial relationship between officials and non-officials, that in Block Panchrukhi, the women leaders were not aware of the development programmes, schemes and projects whereas in Block Rait only about half of the sample population knew about them. It is the duty of the officials to tell the women leaders about such development programmes which they are not fulfilling.

Another interesting fact that came to light was that majority of the respondents of both the blocks did not reply about the interference of state government in the working of P.R.Is. The reason could have been their hesitation or fear to speak against the state government regarding technical knowledge being provided to the P.R.I. leaders. It came to light that in both the blocks, Panchrukhi and Rait, the respondents were not satisfied at all. When the respondents were asked about their satisfaction of level regarding the visits of officials, it was found that in Block Panchrukhi, only one-third of the sample population was satisfied and almost none was happy with the officials frequency of visits. Finally, in this chapter, the issue of satisfaction regarding the control of various departments under P.R.Is. was studied and once again, the respondents did not answer. Thus, the sub-hypothesis, that is the negligence and indifferent attitude of executives towards women leaders have resulted in dissatisfaction amongst them, has been proved correct.

Finally, the last chapter dealt with the participatory role of women leaders in developmental activities. It became clear that women elected representatives of the sample population were not very active in eleimination of purdah system and the same was the case of dowry system's eradication. They were not highly associated with female literacy programmes and at medium level in avoidance of elimination of girl child and reduction of domestic violence. So, it was found that the respondents were socially responsible only at a medium level.

The economic activities were studied from six angles. Firstly, it was found that majority of the respondents participated at a medium level in assisting others in seeking employment whereas the knowledge about the preparation of budget was found to be of a high level in Block Rait but low in Panchrukhi. This can also be attributed to the reason of low level of education. It was also observed that as far as preparation of budget was concerned the women leaders' participation was of a medium level and regarding checking misappropriation of Panchayat budget, the response was definitely of a high level. It was found that they participated only at a medium level while discussing the expenditure of schools, anganwadis, etc. Finally, the role of women leaders in getting the right of parental property was found to be different in both the blocks—Rait and Panchrukhi. In Block Rait, the respondents were not very active and in Block Panchrukhi, the majority involved themselves at an average level.

The next area that was studied was the participatory role of the elected women representatives in educational activities. It was found that a majority of them were highly aware and helped in making the literacy programmes work but while studying the perception of the respondents; it became clear that the contribution of the respondents was low regarding providing education to preschool and primary school children. Basically, this is the problem being faced both by NGOs and the Government, that is, the means to reach out to grass-root women so as to make them aware and alert in bringing about a change in the educational area. The government has attempted programmes through the Ministry of Education like the Mahila Samakhya Programme and an awareness generation programme of the Central Social Welfare Board.

So, the sub-hypothesis, that is, low literacy and lack of knowledge amongst women leaders, have resulted in non-performance of their role has been proved partially as all the indicators in this activity of education was found to be of low or medium level. It was further found that sports or cultural shows and enrolment drive of children in school were also promoted by the elected women representatives at medium level.

The next indicator examined was the involvement of elected women representatives with public work and respondents were found to be highly active in associating themselves with construction of road and drainage facilities in the villages. The high level involvement could be due to the self-interest of developing their respective areas and linking it to the main roads for better market facility and trade. Further, their contribution in installing smokeless chulhas was found to be of a low level. Their role in obtaining drinking water for common people construction of a Community Bhawan was gauged at a medium level. Provision of good hygienic sanitation facilities at public places and construction of pucca houses for down tradden by the elected women representatives was again found to be of an average level.

The last indicator was the study of trade and commerce activities including organization of cooperative marketing of agricultural and other products, providing cheap credit facilities to people, checking malpractices, maintenance of cooperatives godowns, organization of cooperative consumer societies and procurement of remunerative prices. It was noticed that the contribution of the elected women representatives was low. This proves the hypothesis of this study that the women leaders have failed to perform their duties at the grass-root level.

SUGGESTIONS

It is observed that as a "socially and economically disadvantaged section" women have to understand the ways in which power is shared and why greater representation is needed to influence the redistribution of power and resources. Policies of reservation can redress the imbalance of both the genders. Rural development, based on gender equality, can be attained by women themselves by integrating themselves so as to develop and employ their skills. Women's representation is seen as an instrument for change and women are seen as an interest group who will take up the cause of other disadvantaged women. It is anticipated that once they become a part of the decision-making process, they would demand participation in development decisions and a reorientation of public policies. The process of Indian women coming into politics at their own has been slow and halting because Indian culture is apolitical and the force of tradition has been particularly against participation of women in politics.

Based on the findings of the study, following are measures outlined for making full and efficient use of potentials and skills of rural women for accelerating development process:

1. In Article 243 B of the Constitution (73rd Amendment Act) it has been mentioned that Gram Sabha means a body consisting of persons registered in the electoral rolls relating to a village comprised within an Area Panchayat at the Village. According to this provision of the Act, the Panchayats in and around industrial towns are dominated by migrants. The concentration of the local people is sometimes ignored. So, it is suggested that at the time of the creation of a new Panchayat, the local people may be given preference.
2. Since it is given in the provisions of the Constitution that the legislative of state may, by law, endow the Panchayats with such powers and authority as may be necessary to enable them to function as institutions of self-government. This provision creates a disparity in devolution of powers, from one state to another, as every state creates its own parameters of powers and responsibilities that are given to the Panchayats. So, it is suggested that it may be laid down clearly in the Constitution about the powers, authority and

responsibilities so as to avoid any variation from one state to another.

3. Section 7 dealt with the functions of Gram Sabha which outlined amongst other functions about the identification of beneficiaries for the implementation of development schemes pertaining to the village but during the course of study, it was found that most of the elected women representatives were not aware of the development programmes initiated by the State Government from time to time.

   Hence, it is suggested that government should take necessary action to hold workshops, seminars and awareness campaigns so that all members are apprised of them. The elected women representatives spend most of their time in household chores. So, it is evident from the study that they could not devote much time to the functioning of P.R.Is. Since, the women have to do all household work manually; a solution to this problem can be mechanization. The government may provide soft loan or one time grant to elected women representatives to buy electronic household gadgets which will definitely have a positive bearing on their daily schedule thereby enabling them to spare enough time for a meaningful role in the P.R.Is.

4. It was found that the respondents were not satisfied with the technical knowledge provided to them as well as the frequency of the visits of officials. It is suggested here that these officials should come under the direct control and supervision of these elected representatives so as to have a better development process.

5. A discrepancy was found in both the blocks under study regarding their knowledge about the preparation of budget. This shows an unbalanced approach of the officials. This is substantiated by the

fact that out of the total 3,037 number of Gram Panchayats in Himachal Pradesh in which there were 6,074 number of Pradhans and Up-Pradhans, only 4,883 were provided training and 1,191 mumbers of Pradhans and Up-Pradhans were left untrained by the end of March, 2004. Same was the case of Gram Panchayat Members Out of 18,549 members of Gram Panchayat, 7,554 were imparted training whereas 10,995 were left untrained. Although their tenure about to be over, they are still waiting to be trained. It is suggested to set up more Panchayat training camps to ensure 100 per cent coverage and regular training to the Panchayati Raj functionaries.

6. Role of women in children's education is very vital as early socialization of the child takes place mainly in the family under the guidance of the mother. They should be motivated if their children are to be educated. During the course of study, it was observed that the participation of the elected women representatives in providing education to preschool and primary school children was low. So, it is suggested here that the government must promote a higher status of education so as to improve the level of literacy among children in rural areas.
7. In the light of the above, there is an urgent need to make the women leaders literate and acquaint them with their rights and responsibilities. It is suggested that they should be trained to exercise the rights and shoulder the responsibilities in an effective manner. Such training, if not imparted, will not only check the proxy decision, made by men but may sooner or later lead to an overall improvement in the quality of decision-making, thereby, raising the welfare format of the rural society.
8. The trade and commerce activities had a low input from elected women representatives. Actually, the

development of agro-business is quite complicated and needs to be understood by the farmers. The risk and uncertainty must be taken care of. The farmers have to be persuaded to market their crop and produce by providing infrastructural support roads, cold storage chains, godowns, etc.

9. The private entrepreneurs can be encouraged to help in setting up agro-based industries in rural areas. High cost of transport, irregular electric supply, poor genetic quality of the crop, lack of assured market, etc. are the main concerns of farmers. Help can be coordinated and organised by non-governmental organisations.
10. Various programmes for welfare and development of women are integrated for giving the women representatives an opportunity to improve their economic condition and leadership quality.
11. More opportunities of self-employment should be given to womenfolk in the rural areas of Himachal Pradesh.
12. Frequency of visits of officials to P.R.Is. must be increased.
13. The Non-Governmental Organizations, who are getting aid from the government, must come under direct control and guidance of these leaders.
14. Bureaucratic approach should be given up. Bureaucracy should perform the role of non-in test ference in the P.R.I. working and be ecouraging.

The 73rd Amendment of the Indian Constitution and the Himachal Pradesh Panchayati Raj Act, 1994 are not ends in themselves. They made the advent of grass-root democracy in Himachal Pradesh. Many more amendments will be needed in the Constitution and the state legislation from time to time to strengthen it. There is a need for a closer coordination between women's organizations and the elected women representatives to strengthen the struggle of women for equality and justice in the economic, social and political sphere. It is believed that without organised pressure, it would be difficult to get women's issues and perspectives on the political agenda.

BIBLIOGRAPHY

(I) BOOKS

Bandyopadhyay, D. and Mukherjee, Amitava (2004), *New Issues in Panchayati Raj*, Concept Publishing Company, New Delhi.

Banerjee, N. K. (1995), *Grass-root Employment (1975-1990), A Discussion Paper*, Centre for Women's Development Studies, New Delhi.

Bhargava, B.S. (1979) *Panchayati Raj System and Political Parties*, Ashish Publishing House, New Delhi.

Bhargava, B.S. (1979), *Panchayati Raj Institution—An Analysis of Issuess and Recommendations of Asoka Mehta Commission*, Ashish Publishing House, New Delhi.

Bhartwal, C.P. and Kishore Kumkum (2003), *Public Administration in India*, A.P.H. Publishing Corporation, New Delhi.

Bhatnagar, S. (1974), *Panchayati Raj in Kangra District*, Orient Longman, New Delhi.

Biju M. R. (1998), *Dynamics of New Panchayati Raj System*, Kanishka Publishers, New Delhi.

Centre for Women's Development Studies (1986), *The Seeds of Change; Role of Grass-root Rural Women's Organisation in Development*, New Delhi.

Centre for Women's Development Studies (1989), *Partners in Grass-root Democracy*, New Delhi.

Chakraborty, Shanti (1985), *Rural Women's Claim to Priority, Selected Documents from International and Indian Archives 1975-1985*, Centre for Women's Development Studies, New Delhi.

Kohli Shanti Chandra (1997) *A Study of Women in*

Administration Situational Analysis, Radha Publications New Delhi.

Chaudhary, D.S. (1981), *Emerging Rural Leadership in an Indian State*, Manthan Publications, New Delhi.

Chapman, Jane Roberts (1976), *Economic Independence for Women*, Sage Publications, London.

Chatterjee, A. (1975), *A Statistical Profile of Landless Agricultural Women Workers*, Vikas Publications, New Delhi.

Chatterjee, B.B. (Ed.) (1969), *Micro Studies in Community Development, Panchayati Raj and Cooperation*, Sterling Publications, New Delhi.

Chaturvedi, T.N. (1981), *Panchayati Raj*, Indian Institute of Public Administration, New Delhi.

Choksi, H.P. (1971), *A Study of Mobilization of Resources for Village Panchayat in Baroda District*, Planning Commission, New Delhi.

Danda, A.K. (1984), *Studies on Rural Development—Experiences and Issues*, Inter-India Publications, New Delhi.

Desai, K.S. (1962), *Panchayati Raj*, Asia Publishing House, Bombay.

Desai, Neera (1974), *Women in Modern India*, Vora and Company, Bombay.

Desai, Neera (1987), *Women and Society in India*, Ajanta Publishing Company, New Delhi.

Dey, S.K. (1986), *Panchayati Raj in Independent India: Some Personal Reflections*, Institute of Social Sciences and Concept, New Delhi.

Dutta, Nikunjalata (1989), *Village Panchayats in India: A Case Study of Assam*, New Delhi.

Etzioni, Amitai (1978), *Modern Organizations*, Prentice-Hall of India Pvt. Ltd., New Delhi.

Flammang Janet A. (1984), *Political Women—Current Roles in State and Social Government*, Sage Publications Inc., U.S.

Gaekwad, V.R. (1969), *Panchayati Raj And Bureaucracy—A Study of Relationship Patterns*, NICD, Hyderabad.

Gandhi, M.K. (1953), *Panchayati Raj*, Compiled by R.K. Prabhu, Navjeevan Publishing Co., Ahmedabad.

George, Jacob (ed.), (1967), *Readings on Panchayati Raj*, National Institute of Community Development, Hyderabad.

Goel, S.L. And Rajneesh Shalini (2003), *Panchayati Raj in India, Theory and Practice*, Deep and Deep Publications Pvt. Ltd., New Delhi.

Gupta, Ranjit (1965), *Panchayati Raj in Punjab: A Preliminary Draft on Constitution, Organisation, History and Present Position*, All India Panchayat Parishad Place.

Gupta Sen and Graon C. (1985), *Development Alternative with Women for a New Era: Development Crisis and Alternative Visions*, Earthscan Publishing Co., London.

Hargopal, G. (1980), *Administrative Leadership and Rural Development in India*, Light and Life Publishers, New Delhi.

Jain, L.C. et al. (1985), *Grass Without Roads: Rural Government Under Auspices*, Sage Publications, New Delhi.

Kothari, Shanti and Roy, Ramashray (1981), *Relations Between Politicians and Administrators at the District Level*, Indian Institute of Public Administration, New Delhi.

Himachal Pradesh (1953), *Himachal Pradesh Mein Panchayati Raj*, Shimla.

Inamdar, N.R. (1970), *Functioning of Village Panchayats*, Popular Publishing House, Bombay.

Indian Institute of Public Administration (1972), *Case Studies in Panchayati Raj*, New Delhi.

Kasturi, Leela (1995), *Development, Patriarchy and Politics: Indian Women in the Political Process, 1947-1992*, Centre for Women's Development Studies, New Delhi.

Kaur, Satnam (1987), *Women in Rural Development: A Case Study*, Mittal Publications, New Delhi.

Khan, M.Z. and Sharma, Kamlesh (1982), *Profile of a Nyaya Panchayat*, National Publishing Company, New Delhi.

Khanna, Ratan Lal (1956), *Panchayati Raj in India: A Comparative Study*, English Book Depot, Chandigarh.

Khanna R.L. (1966), *Panchayati Raj in Punjab,* Mohindra Capital Publishers, Chandigarh.

Khanna, R.L. (1972), *Panchayati Raj in India*, English Book Depot, Ambala.

Krishnan, M.G. (1990), *Panchayati Raj in India*, Mittal Publishing House, New Delhi.

Kushwaha, R. (1977), *Working of Nyaya Panchayats in India: A Case Study of Varanasi District*, Young Asia Publishing House, New Delhi.

Maddick, Henry (1970), *Panchayati Raj: A Study of Rural Local Government*, Longmans Green, London.

Maheshwari, B. (1963), *Studies in Panchayati Raj*, Metropolitan, New Delhi.

Mahajan, K. Sanjeev (1984), "Some Aspects of Personal Management in the Kangra Central Cooperation Bank Limited With Special Reference to Dharamshala Head Office", Unpublished Dissertation Submitted to Department of Public Administration, Panjab University, Chandigarh.

Majumdar, A.K. and Singh, Bhanwar (1997), *Historical and Conceptual Development of Panchayati Raj*, Radha Publications, New Delhi.

Manikhyamka, P. (1989), *Women in Panchayati Raj Structures*, Gian Publishing House, New Delhi.

Mathai, John (1983), *Village Government in British India*, Neeraj Publishing House, New Delhi.

Mathur, M.V. et al. (1966), *Panchayati Raj in Rajasthan: A Case Study in Jaipur District*, Impex India, New Delhi.

Mathur, M.V. and Narain, Iqbal (1969), *Panchayati Raj, Planning and Democracy,* Asia Publishing House, Bombay.

Mazumdar, Vina (1998), *Peasant Women Organize for Empowerment—The Bankura Experiment*, Centre for Women's Development Studies, New Delhi.

Mehta, Balwantrai (1978), *Report of the Committee on Panchayati Raj Institutions,* Ministry of Agriculture and Irrigation, New Delhi.

Mishra, S.N. (1979), *Politics and Leadership in Municipal Government*, Inter-India Publications, Delhi.

Mishra, S.N. (1989), *New Horizons in Rural Development Administration*, Mittal Publications New Delhi.

Mishra, S.N. and Singh, S.S. (1993), *Roads to Model Panchayati Raj*, Mittal Publications, New Delhi.

Narain, Iqbal (1970), *Panchayati Raj Administration Old Control and New Challenges*, Indian Institute of Public Administration, New Delhi.

Oakley, Peter et al. (1991), *Projects with People Development*, Oxford and IBH Publishing Pvt. Co., New Delhi.

Palanithurai, G. (1953), *New Panchayati Raj System at Work—An Evaluation*, Concept Publishing Company, New Delhi.

Palanithurai G., Dwarki, B.R. and Narayanaswamy, S. (1977), *Major Issues in New Panchayati Raj System*, Kanishka Publishers, New Delhi.

Prasad, R.C. (1971), *Democracy and Development*, Rachna Prakashan, New Delhi.

Rangrajan, C.I. (2004), Chairman of the Finance Commission, www. Orissagov. Nic.in/Panchayat fiscal.html.

Retzlaff, H. Ralph (1962), *Village Government in India*, Asia Publishing House, Bombay.

Satyanarayana, P. (1990), *Towards New Panchayati Raj—Critical Perspectives on the Reorganization of Rural Local Government*, Uppal Publishing House, New Delhi.

Sharma, Kumud, (1998), *Power vs. Representation*, Centre for Women's Development Studies, New Delhi.

Sharma, S.K. and Malhotra, S.L. (1977), *Integrated Rural Development—Approach Strategy and Perspectives*, Abhinav Publications, New Delhi.

Singh, Seema (2003), *Panchayati Raj and Women Empowerment*, Ocean Books Pvt. Ltd., New Delhi.

Usha Rao, N.J. (1985), *Women in Developing Society*, Ashish Publishing House, New Delhi.

The Tribune, Chandigarh, (September 7, 2001).

Tomar, B.S. (1991), *Panchayati Raj in India—Literature on Features Trends and Prospects*, Indian Bibliographic Bureau, Delhi.

(II) ARTICLES

Abraham, A.S. (22nd May, 1989), "Securing Panchayati Raj: A Double Ended Message", *Times of India*, New Delhi.

Adisehian, Maleon (26th January, 1980), "Panchayati Raj: Malady and Remedy", *Yojana*, New Delhi.

Agarwal, V.C. (18th November, 1988), "Panchayati Raj: New Awareness", *Economic Times*, New Delhi.

Balasubramanyam, Vinal (11th May, 1985) "What and Why of Women's Studies", *Mainstream*, New Delhi.

Banerjee, N. K. (1995), "Grass-root Empowerment (1975-1990)", A Discussion Paper, Centre for Women's Development Studies, New Delhi.

Bapuji, M. (27th December, 1975), "Panchayati Raj in Tribal Areas", *Mainstream* New Delhi.

Bhargava, B.S. (March 1987), "Panchayati Raj Reforms in Karnataka", *Panchayat Sandesh*.

Bora, D.S. (12th April, 1973), "Why Panchayati Raj does not Work?", *Hindustan Times*, New Delhi.

Centre for Women's Development Studies (24th August, 1989), *"Parents in Grass-root Democracy"*, New Delhi.

Darda, R.S. (May, 1973), "Panchayati Raj in Rajasthan", *Kurukshetra*, New Delhi.

Jain, Devaki, (27th April, 1985), "Role of Women in Development", *Mainstream*, New Delhi.

Fritz, Dan (April-June, 1973), "Evolution of Official and Non-Official Roles in Mysore State and Panchayati Raj" *Indian Journal of Public Administration*, Vol. 19, Indian Institute of Public Administration, New Delhi.

Gada, C.R. (1977), "Emerging Patterns of Rural Leadership—A Case Study in Gulbarga District" *Indian Journal of Public Administration*, Vol. 23, Indian Institute of Public Administration, New Delhi.

Gowda, Govinda S and Dhadave, M.S. (1998), "Political Linkage of Women Leaders of Panchayati Raj Institutions: An Empirical Evidence from Karnataka", *Administrative Change,* Vol. XXX, No. 2 and Vol. XXVI, No. 1), Centre for Administrative Change, Jaipur.

Kitchlu, T.N. (15th November, 1991), "Women's Rights: Legislative Measures", *Yojana*, New Delhi.

Kopchar, J. and Pandya, R.D. (March 1992), "Status of Women in India", *Kurukshetra*, New Delhi.

Mahajan, Sanjeev K. (January-December, 2004), "Public Accountability of State Level Undertakings in India—A Case Study" *Dynamics of Public Administration,* Department of Public Administration, University of Lucknow, Lucknow.

Mishra, S.N. (1977), "Characteristics of Emerging Leadership in Rural India, A Case Study in a Bihar Panchayat" in *Indian Journal of Public Administration*, Vol. 23, Indian Institute of Public Administration, New Delhi.

Narain, Iqbal (July-September, 1966), "The Administration Challenge to Panchayati Raj", *Indian Journal of Public Administration*, Vol. XII, Indian Institute of Public Administration, New Delhi.

Panda, Snehlata (October-December, 1996) "Emerging Pattern of Leadership Among Rural Women in Orissa" *Indian Journal of Public Administration*, Vol. XIII No. 4, Indian Institute of Public Administration, New Delhi.

Panda, Snehlata (January-March 1999) "Political Empowerment of Women; Case of Orissa P.R.Is.", *Indian Journal of Public Administration,* Vol. XLV, No. 1, Indian Institute of Public Administration, New Delhi.

Pandha, Sunita (October, 1988), "Women's Studies and Women's Movement" *Economic and Political Weekly*, Bombay.

Patel, Thirty D. (1984), "Panchayati Raj: An Overview", in Rajput, R.S. and Meghe, D.R. (eds.), *Panchayati Raj in India: Democracy at Grass roots*, Deep and Deep Publishing

Co., New Delhi.

Patil, R.K. (1984), "Plea for Village Self-Government" in Rajput R.S. and Meghe, D.R. (eds.), *Panchayati Raj in India: Democracy at Grass roots*, Deep and Deep Publishing Co., New Delhi.

Reddy, Narayana G. (2nd November, 1985), "Women's Role in Economy and Society", *Mainstream*, New Delhi.

Sharma, Kumud (1988), "Power vs. Representation—Feminist Dilemmas, Ambivalent State and the Debate on Reservation for Women in India", Centre for Women's Development Studies, New Delhi.

Singh, Sita Ram (1996), "Revitalization of Panchayats", *Kurukshetra*, Vol. XXXIX, No. 6, New Delhi.

Vepa, K. Ram (April-June, 1962), "Official Non-Official Relations in Panchayati Raj—The Experience of Andhra Pradesh", *Indian Journal of Public Administration*, Vol. VII. No. 2, Institute of Public Administration, New Delhi.

(III) REPORTS

Economics and Statistics Department (1999), *Brief Facts: Himachal Pradesh*, Shimla.

Census of India, 1991.

Census of India, 2001.

Government of Himachal Pradesh (1994), *Panchayati Raj Act*, Directorate of Panchayati Raj, Shimla.

Government of Himachal Pradesh (1996-2001), *Annual Administrative Reports*, Department of Panchayati Raj, Shimla.

Government of India, (1961), *Third Five Year Plan*, Planning Commission, New Delhi.

Government of India (1974), "Towards Equality", *Report of the Committee on the Status of Women in India*, Department of Social Welfare, Ministry of Education and Social Welfare, New Delhi.

Government of India (1988), *National Perspective Plan for Women 1988-2000 A.D.*, Department of Women and

Child Development, Ministry of Human Resources Development, New Delhi.

Government of India (1998), *Report of the Committee on Panchayati Raj Institutions*, Ministry of Agriculture and Irrigation Development, New Delhi.

National Perspective Plan for Women (1988-2000), *A Perspective from the Women's Movement: Report of a Debate*, New Delhi.

Report of the Team for the Study of Community Projects and National Extension Service (1957).

Seventy-third Constitutional Amendment Act, 1992, Ministry of Law, Justice and Company Affairs (Legislative Department), New Delhi.

INDEX